4⁰⁰

Everyman, I will go with thee,
and be thy guide

H

**THE EVERYMAN
LIBRARY**

*The Everyman Library was founded by J. M. Dent
in 1906. He chose the name Everyman because he wanted
to make available the best books ever written in every
field to the greatest number of people at the cheapest possible
price. He began with Boswell's 'Life of Johnson';
his one-thousandth title was Aristotle's 'Metaphysics',
by which time sales exceeded forty million.*

*Today Everyman paperbacks remain true to
J. M. Dent's aims and high standards, with a wide range
of titles at affordable prices in editions which address
the needs of today's readers. Each new text is reset to give
a clear, elegant page and to incorporate the latest thinking
and scholarship. Each book carries the pilgrim logo,
the character in 'Everyman', a medieval morality play,
a proud link between Everyman
past and present.*

VIRGIN LIVES
AND HOLY DEATHS

Two Exemplary Biographies for Anglo-Norman Women

THE LIFE OF ST CATHERINE
THE LIFE OF ST LAWRENCE

Translated with introductions and notes by
JOCELYN WOGAN-BROWNE
University of Liverpool

and

GLYN S. BURGESS
University of Liverpool

EVERYMAN
J. M. DENT · LONDON
CHARLES E. TUTTLE
VERMONT

Introduction, translations, notes and other critical apparatus
© J M Dent 1996

This edition first published in 1996
All rights reserved

J. M. Dent
Orion Publishing Group
Orion House, 5 Upper St Martin's Lane,
London WC2H 9EA
and
Charles E. Tuttle Co., Inc.
28 South Main Street,
Rutland, Vermont 05701, USA

Typeset in Sabon by CentraCet Ltd, Cambridge
Printed in Great Britain by
The Guernsey Press Co. Ltd, Guernsey, C. I.

British Library Cataloguing-in-Publication Data
is available upon request.

ISBN 0 460 87580 9

CONTENTS

Note on the Translators vii
Acknowledgements viii
Abbreviations ix
Introduction xi
  Saints' Lives xi
  Women, Saints and Saints' Lives xiv
  Virgin Martyrs and Medieval Women xvii
  The Life of St Catherine *by Clemence of Barking* xix
    St Catherine xix
    The Life of St Catherine: *author, date, and*
      manuscripts xxiii
    Provenance and milieu xxiv
    Sources and influences xxvii
    Treatment xxix
  The Life of St Lawrence xxxv
    St Lawrence xxxv
    The Life of St Lawrence: *date and manuscripts* xxxviii
    Sources xxxix
    Treatment xl
  Style xliii
Suggestions for Further Reading lx
Note on the Texts lxiv

VIRGIN LIVES AND HOLY DEATHS 1

The Life of St Catherine 3
The Life of St Lawrence 45

Commentary 61
  St Catherine 61

St Lawrence 79
Appendix 93
  Extracts from The Life of St Catherine 93
  Extracts from The Life of St Lawrence 100
Indexes of Proper Names 105

NOTE ON THE TRANSLATORS

JOCELYN WOGAN-BROWNE did degrees at the Universities of Melbourne and Oxford, and is a Senior Lecturer at the University of Liverpool. She has published numerous articles on women and earlier literature in Britain. With Bella Millett (University of Southampton) she has edited *Medieval English Prose for Women: Selections from the Katherine Group and Ancrene Wisse* (Oxford: Oxford University Press, 1990; repr. 1992). She has edited a tape anthology, *Voicing Medieval Women* (forthcoming, Chaucer Studio), and she is currently working on a study, *Authorized Virgins: The Literature of Female Celibacy in Medieval England, c.1150–c.1350*, for Oxford University Press. She is a founder-member of the Gender and Medieval Studies (UK) research group and a board member of the Anglo-Norman Text Society.

GLYN S. BURGESS studied French at St John's College, Oxford. He then took his MA at McMaster University, Hamilton, Ontario, and went on to do a doctorate at the Sorbonne. He has taught at Queen's University, Kingston, Ontario, at the University of South Carolina and, since 1971, at the University of Liverpool, where he is currently Professor of French and head of the department. He has translated the *Song of Roland* for Penguin Classics and has published widely on twelfth-century courtly literature, especially on the *Lais* of Marie de France, which he has translated, also for Penguin Classics, in collaboration with Professor Keith Busby (University of Oklahoma). He has been associated since its inception in the mid-1970s with the International Courtly Literature Society, of which he was President from 1989 to 1995.

ACKNOWLEDGEMENTS

We owe a great debt to Professor William MacBain, who generously read the draft typescript of our translation of Clemence of Barking and made many improvements. Dr Leslie Brook kindly undertook the same service for the *Life of St Lawrence*. Students on courses in Medieval Women's Writing at Liverpool have helped us with much stimulating discussion and comment. We are grateful to Janet McArthur, Julia Bagguley and Nicholas Watson for reading and commenting on the introduction. Part of the work was supported by a Fellowship awarded to Jocelyn Wogan-Browne at the Humanities Research Centre in the Australian National University, Canberra, for which we thank the directors of the Centre and the University. Like most people involved with Anglo-Norman texts in Britain, we have been encouraged in our work by Professor Ian Short and are grateful to him for his inspiration in all matters Anglo-Norman, and in particular for permission to publish extracts from the original texts of the *Life of St Catherine* and the *Life of St Lawrence*, both published by the Anglo-Norman Text Society. We are grateful to Dr Jennifer Fellows for her skilful and patient copy-editing and to Hilary Laurie for her enterprise in publishing this volume.

ABBREVIATIONS

AND	*Anglo-Norman Dictionary*, ed. Louise W. Stone, William Rothwell, *et al.* (London: Modern Humanities Research Association, 1977–92)
ANTS	Anglo-Norman Text Society
Batt	Catherine Batt, 'Clemence of Barking's Transformations of *courtoisie* in *La vie de sainte Catherine d'Alexandrie*', in *Translation in the Middle Ages*, ed. Roger Ellis (*New Comparisons*, 12 (1991), pp. 102–23).
Cabrol and Leclercq	F. M. Cabrol and H. M. Leclercq, *Dictionnaire d'archéologie chrétienne et de liturgie* (Paris: Letouzey et Ane, 1907–53)
CFMA	Classiques français du moyen âge
Delehaye	H. Delehaye, 'Recherches sur le légendier romain. La passion de S. Polychronius', *Analecta Bollandiana*, 51 (1933), 34–98
EETS, ES	Early English Text Society, Extra Series
EETS, OS	Early English Text Society, Original Series
EETS, SS	Early English Text Society, Supplementary Series
Farmer	D. H. Farmer, *The Oxford Dictionary of Saints* (Oxford: Clarendon Press, 1978)
HBS	Henry Bradshaw Society
Katerine	*Seinte Katerine*, ed. S. R. T. O. d'Ardenne and E. J. Dobson, EETS, SS 7 (Oxford: Oxford University Press for the EETS, 1981), pp. 2–131

MacBain	William MacBain, ed., *The Life of St. Catherine by Clemence of Barking*, ANTS 18 (Oxford: Blackwell for the ANTS, 1964)
MRTS	Medieval and Renaissance Texts and Studies
ODCC	*The Oxford Dictionary of the Christian Church*, ed. F. L. Cross and E. A. Livingstone (London, New York and Toronto: Oxford University Press, 1957; 2nd edn 1974)
Passion	Latin passion of St Lawrence, from *Passio SS. Xysti et Laurentii*, ed. in Delehaye, pp. 80–93
PL	*Patrologiae cursus completus . . . series Latina*, ed. J.-P. Migne (Paris, various years)
RS	Rolls Series
Russell	*La vie de saint Laurent: An Anglo-Norman Poem of the Twelfth Century*, ed. D. W. Russell, ANTS 34 (London: ANTS, 1976)
VCH	*Victoria County History of England*
Vulgate	*Passio Sancte Katerine virginis et martyris*, ed. in *Katerine*, pp. 132–203
Ziolkowski	*Nigel of Canterbury: The Passion of St Lawrence, Epigrams and Marginal Poems*, ed. and trans. Jan M. Ziolkowski (Leiden, New York and Cologne: Brill, 1994)

INTRODUCTION

Saints' Lives

The two texts translated in this volume, the *Life of St Catherine* and the *Life of St Lawrence*, belong to the large number of saints' lives which circulated throughout Europe in the Middle Ages and beyond. Written both in Latin and in the various vernacular languages, these texts form part of the genre known as hagiography, 'the writing of the sacred'. *Catherine* and *Lawrence* were composed in the twelfth century in Anglo-Norman, the French written and spoken in England after the Norman Conquest. The *Life of St Catherine* is the only account of this saint written in England which is known to be by a woman (the next life of Catherine certainly by a woman in north-west Europe is by Christine de Pizan in her *City of Ladies* of 1405). The *Life of St Lawrence* portrays male martyrdom and was written at the request of a woman. The life of a saint manifests the sacred on earth through relics and through places associated with the saint as well as through written legends.[1] Since even the smallest relic carries the power of the saint as a whole, a phial of the oil exuded by St Catherine's body on Mount Sinai, or a piece of St Lawrence's gridiron marked with the grease from his roasted flesh, offers contact with the full power of the saint's triumphant integrity. By a similar logic, the text of a saint's life was often understood in the Middle Ages as a form of relic, and an attentive reading or hearing of a saint's legend was seen as a form of actual contact with the saint.[2] Around seventy Anglo-Norman saints' lives in verse have been preserved. As with earlier and later saints' lives, they offer contact with the power and charisma of the saints and also provide a rich and varied corpus of biography. Since saints were powerful intercessors, the needs and aspirations of their communities were often reflected in the retelling of their lives. In them we can see powerful cultural and social models for medieval men and women.

Vernacular saints' lives had wide currency in the Middle Ages. Though many of the extant manuscripts containing saints' lives belonged to monastic houses, they are also found in manuscripts in secular ownership and in the company of secular texts such as lyric poems and romances. This suggests that they were enjoyed by lay audiences.[3] Certainly, the texts of private prayers and devotions to the saints were copied and recopied in manuscript books owned both by Anglo-Norman aristocratic houses and by urban elites. Saints figured in the illuminations of psalters and in the books of hours which provided the basic texts by which laypeople and religious women could perform their private devotions. In addition to such private (though not necessarily silent) reading, medieval men and women might also have heard saints' lives in more public contexts: church preaching and readings, readings to groups in households and in monastic houses, recitations at feasts, the reading aloud of women to their companions and servants, and so on. Saints' lives are often theatrical and dramatic narratives, designed for effective oral delivery.

Like the contemporary narratives of courtly and chivalric romance, many saints' lives in the twelfth and thirteenth centuries are concerned with the formation of personal and social identity and the disposition of dynastic and territorial resources. In the question of whether saints continue their lineage or celibately commit themselves to God, the interests of church and family may coincide or radically divide. Sexuality is a major concern in saints' lives, both as a matter of personal choice and for its implications for kinship and society. Even the narratives of virgin women saints like St Catherine are informed by the structures of family romance, with the difference that the saint is pledged to Christ, the highest-ranking and most handsome bridegroom of all. The narrative structures of saints' lives thus straddle heaven and earth. Pagan suitors and tyrants attempt to compel martyrs to the assent and compliance which they freely give to their true lord and bridegroom in heaven. In saints' lives, earthly relations of power and desire are versions of their heavenly prototypes. The saint's desire for and imitation of God is a true reflection, and the pagan's desire for the saint and exercise of secular power a parodic distortion. These processes of desire and resistance are often represented in stylized and graphic accounts of interrogation, debate and torture. But, however apparently sensational their material, saints' lives, with their dual focus on heaven and earth, and all the entailed possibilities of reflection and distortion between the two, can offer powerful and rich accounts of psychic and social structures.

Saints' lives are also concerned in distinctive ways with the body, as one might expect in a genre so largely founded on the martyrs' imitation of Christ's passion. In their passions saints are repeatedly tortured and dismembered, and in their cults their bodies are fragmented and distributed as relics. Saintly bodies remain unharmed or are triumphantly reconstituted after torture, and so they function as powerful signs of integrity and wholeness, of triumph over dismemberment and death. The *Guide for Anchoresses*, a famous early thirteenth-century text written for well-born young women, links St Lawrence 'on the gridiron' with 'innocent maidens who have their breasts torn off, are whirled to pieces on wheels and have their heads cut off'. Such saints, the *Guide* argues, are like spoilt children with rich fathers who 'wantonly tear up their clothes in order to have new ones': the flesh we receive from Adam can readily be torn up and sacrificed like so much old clothing when our rich father God provides us with a glorious new body at the resurrection.[4] The more beaten and dismembered the martyr, the more powerful the triumph over death, and the more insistently the permanent, glorious body of the resurrection is signalled.

That saints were often more exemplary than imitable did not prevent them from acting as role models. Their achievements and powers mapped out for their audiences both social sanctions and possibilities of personal growth. The pair of biographies offered here – a female saint's life written *by* a woman, and a male saint's martyrdom written *for* a woman – enables us to see something of ideals and actualities in post-Conquest Britain, mediated through saints in this most prolific of narrative forms.

Women, Saints and Saints' Lives

Saints' lives form the bulk of the vernacular writings currently known to be by women in twelfth- and thirteenth-century Britain. One woman writer from this period, Marie de France, is well known to modern audiences: vernacular saints' lives give us three further narrative texts composed by women.[5] In addition to Clemence of Barking's *St Catherine*, there is extant an anonymous nun's twelfth-century life of Edward the Confessor and a thirteenth-century life of the Anglo-Saxon princess Etheldreda, foundress and first abbess of Ely. In this biography Etheldreda becomes 'la reine seinte Audrée', the holy Queen Audrey: the writer of the life gives her own name as Marie and probably lived at Chatteris Abbey.[6]

Whether they were writing a biography of a contemporary, refurbishing a Latin life of an established saint, or popularizing universal saints in the vernacular for the instruction of the faithful, most hagiographers were male clerics, and most saints were men. Women's access to the career structures of the church, to its institutional resources and to its processes of representation was much more limited. It was rarer for women to be canonized than for men, and the centralized procedures for canonization in Rome, which developed in the late twelfth and early thirteenth centuries, made it no easier. Popes, prelates, kings, hermits, bishops, monastic scholars and lay noblemen continued to be added to national and regional calendars of saints, in which early church martyrs, ecclesiastical leaders and major theologians had long been celebrated as universal saints of the church. New biographies were written for the new male medieval saints. But only a very small number of women became saints in the Middle Ages, though a slightly larger number achieved recognition as holy women in their communities without being officially canonized.[7] No life of a contemporary medieval woman composed by a woman is known to survive from twelfth- or thirteenth-century Britain, unless we assume the biography of Christina of Markyate (c. 1097–c. 1161) to have been dictated by Christina herself as a basis for the Latin life now extant.[8] Women were in general more likely to be in a position to hear, read, commission or imitate a saintly life than to become a saint or to write hagiography. Even aristocratic women would not necessarily expect to write as well as read: this was delegated to the clerks and clerics they employed. Writing was not a skill indissociable from literacy, and hence was something few women or laymen practised to any extent.[9]

Though women were in many ways under-represented in saints' lives, the genre was nonetheless important to them. Upper-class women were sometimes patrons for saints' lives, as well as commissioners and owners of devotional manuscripts, just as they were patrons (and in some cases foundresses) of monastic houses and other religious institutions dedicated to particular saints.[10] In the earlier Middle Ages, the women chiefly involved in the production of hagiography were queens and abbesses. The life of St Margaret of Scotland (1046–93), for example, was written for her daughter Matilda, who was the first wife of Henry I.[11] Like her mother and many of the Norman and Angevin royal women, Matilda was a literate and influential patron. Margaret was one of the last members of the Anglo-Saxon royal family, and, together with Edward the Confessor of England (d. 1066), she was promoted as a saint in the twelfth and thirteenth centuries. Her daughter had both a dynastic and a personal interest in commissioning her mother's biography. In the twelfth and thirteenth centuries there is more evidence for the direct involvement of women from a slightly wider, though still restricted, class range. Countess Isabella of Arundel (d. before 1282) seems to have been the patron of Latin and vernacular biographies of medieval Anglo-Norman church-men.[12] Christina of Markyate was a foundress and prioress. She was the daughter of Huntingdon parents, who seem to have belonged to the lower ranks of the nobility. She won acceptance from the monks of St Albans as a holy woman and was given the Latin biography mentioned above, though she was not canonized.[13] St Margaret of Scotland remained the only British woman of the period to be both canonized and given a full hagiographic biography in twelfth- or thirteenth-century Britain. In stories of shrine cures, miracles, pilgrimages and relics, there can be seen a still wider socio-economic range of women's interests (both ascribed and actual) in saints' cults and their texts. In its twelfth-century development, for instance, the cult of St Margaret of Antioch turned a virgin martyr into the patroness of childbirth: text amulets of St Margaret were worn in labour by upper- and lower-class women alike, and the life of the saint was sometimes read aloud to them.[14]

Women's interests in the biographies of churchmen, kings and other male saints could be satisfied either from older or from contemporary medieval models. For female biography, the range was narrower. Apart from lives of earlier medieval British queens and abbesses, the ranks of women saints were chiefly filled by the early and often legendary or semi-legendary female martyrs of the universal church. These figures were regularly celebrated in the Latin liturgy, and rewritings of their lives form the largest category of female saintly biography represented in post-Conquest Britain. The virgin martyr is so dominant a figure of female sanctity that lives of other women were written as far as possible in conformity with the conventions of this type of legend. For instance, if a woman saint had been married, her marriage was presented as chaste, if not actually virginal. Chaste spiritual marriage itself was a contemporary ideal in this period and was propagated by the church, and in certain circumstances by royal families.[15]

The three Anglo-Norman lives written by women all concern virgin saints. Catherine was a newly important virgin martyr, whose passion was supposed to have occurred in the fourth century, though her cult dated from the eleventh. Etheldreda (Audrey in the Anglo-Norman life by Marie), was, as the Venerable Bede had claimed in his influential eighth-century life of her, twice married, once widowed, once separated, and still a virgin when she became an abbess.[16] Virginity is also the major feature of the anonymous nun's life of Edward the Confessor. The claim that his childless marriage had been a saintly virgin one was important for his widow Edith, when she commissioned an early Latin biography of her husband. It continued to be important to the Angevin royal house in the late twelfth century. Edward could be presented as a powerful and saintly predecessor, whose virgin marriage converted a potential political liability into spiritual fecundity and also explained gaps in the succession of Anglo-Saxon and Norman kings. Virginity in saints was highly valued for its intercessory power with God, but it was also an ideal with social and behavioural implications, particularly for women.

Virgin Martyrs and Medieval Women

For the Middle Ages, virginity was not a negative state but a condition of ardent attachment to God. Virginity, or at least celibacy, was an important ideal for men as well as women: its practice was actively demanded from monks and from churchmen from the eleventh century onwards. In its somewhat different female form, virginity was a spiritual and cultural ideal with implications for a wide range of women, and not only for vowed and consecrated virgins and other women religious. Just as the figure of the Virgin Mary provided an inimitable but powerful model, through which cultural demands were mediated not only to nuns but to mothers, wives and widows, so too the virgin martyr offered an ideal to which other representations of female sanctity were aligned.

In ranking virginity as the most valuable form of sanctity, hagiography offered women both problems and opportunities. Figures such as St Etheldreda of Ely might strongly exemplify virginity or at least chastity as the ideal condition in marriage, but this was seldom a practical option. Few women, other than wealthy widows of rank, were in a position to dispose of their own sexuality and fecundity, let alone to withhold it in marriage. On the other hand, sexually active saints such as Mary Magdalen, Mary of Egypt and Thaïs, were saintly because they had repented: their lives offered an ambivalent example of female sexual activity followed by long years of harsh penance and asceticism.[17]

Only at the end of the thirteenth century, with the translation into Anglo-Norman of the life of Countess Elisabeth of Hungary (d. 1231), was a biological mother and contemporary medieval woman fully recognized as a saint in a vernacular life. (Fierce penitential asceticism remained a hallmark of Elisabeth's sanctity, however, and she was a saint in spite, rather than because, of her maternity.[18] As late as the fifteenth century, Margery Kempe's concern that God might not love married women as well as he did virgins continues to indicate the problems which ideal virgin sanctity created for wives and mothers. Yet Kempe's dialogue with God on this subject shows a wife and mother actively negotiating for the status and rank of virgin. This suggests that it remained more useful to achieve accommodation to the powerful stereotype of the virgin saint than to reject it.[19]

Virgin martyrs such as Cecilia, Agnes, Agatha, Margaret and Catherine exemplified aristocratic and beautiful virgin heroines. For the twelfth and later centuries, the narratives of their passions retained their cultural function as sacred history, but they were also important as spiritual romance. In saints' lives of this period, even more than in earlier biographies, the virginity or chastity of a female saint is constructed as a form of ideal marriage to Christ. As much as any courtly romance heroine, the virgin is a nuptial figure, and her narrative destiny is union with her bridegroom. This union takes place beyond death, in the heavenly court or bower to which these brides of Christ look as they make their final prayers before decapitation. Death in this genre is the equivalent of marriage in romance. It signals the appropriate happy ending, which is the beginning of the heroine's new life. In this, as in other ways, there are potentially very interesting parallels between medieval uses of virgin martyrs as romance heroines and some modern secular forms of romance. Questions about how far cultural linkages between represented female constancy, nuptiality, torture and death can be seen as useful or acceptable have been debated in modern accounts of hagiography, as they have in discussion of some modern narrative genres. In the case of such powerful role-models as romance heroines, whether medieval or modern, the question of what the virgin exemplifies for her audiences is not trivial. The virgin-martyr passion has been recently seen both as a form of rape fantasy and as a genre offering eloquent heroines and a version of personal autonomy to women.[20]

The evidence of medieval women's own engagement with the saints and their biographies is less well known from Britain in the twelfth and thirteenth centuries than from continental or fourteenth- and fifteenth-century British evidence. However, the post-Conquest evidence suggests a complicated and varying picture in which women do not have to be seen as only passive or collusive victims. On the one hand, for example, medieval treatises often recommended mortification of the flesh as a 'martyrdom without iron', which would enable women to imitate the heroism of the virgin martyrs. There is evidence – warnings to women against cutting off pieces of their own flesh or against using unorthodox or over-severe methods of flagellation – to suggest that some women, especially enclosed women religious, could internalize such injunctions to an alarming extent.[21] On the other hand, medieval women sometimes interpreted virgin-martyr passions as useful precedents for themselves. Christina of Markyate, before she escaped to her religious career, was threatened with marital rape after a betrothal forced on her by her parents. She recounted to her bridegroom the story of St Cecilia, a fourth-century virgin martyr who, on her wedding-night, converted her Roman husband to Christianity and a vow of chaste marriage. There can be little doubt that the precedent of virgin-martyr saints provided Christina with an important example and a source of strength in her protracted (and ultimately successful) struggle for a religious career.[22] Against this background and in the light of these possibilities, the life of St Catherine by a learned and highly articulate medieval woman is of particular significance, while the life of St Lawrence offers the thought-provoking spectacle of a male saint, stripped and tortured in a passion designed to serve 'as an example' (*Lawrence* v. 79) for a female audience.

The Life of St Catherine *by Clemence of Barking*

St Catherine

Catherine of Alexandria is the pre-eminent virgin martyr, widely venerated throughout Europe, and, together with Mary Magdalen, Lawrence, Margaret and George, one of the most popular saints in Britain.[23] Important as she is, however, Catherine's legend has little historical basis, and her feast-day, long celebrated on 25 November, was excised by the Vatican from the Roman Catholic calendar of saints in 1969. Although she was supposedly martyred in fourth-century Alexandria, the story of her passion first occurs in Greek accounts from the ninth century, and there are few records of her cult in the Latin West before the eleventh century. Catherine (her name comes from the Greek *katharos*, 'pure') is nevertheless a particularly forceful and eloquent version of the virgin martyr. In her legend, she lives autonomously as the orphan daughter and heir of a king, in charge of her own household. She directly challenges the Emperor Maxentius over his animal sacrifices to pagan idols. Her thorough classical education and formidable learning are then deployed in public debate with Maxentius' philosophers, whom she defeats and converts. In her dungeon she is visited by Christ himself. She converts the emperor's wife and the captain of his guard and refuses Maxentius' offer of marriage and of a statue of herself to be worshipped. As a specially horrific form of torture, a machine of knife-studded wheels is devised for her, but she remains undismayed and unharmed. In the event, the wheel is shattered by angels before it touches her. Catherine continues to sustain and inspire her converts as they are executed at the command of the outraged emperor. When Catherine herself is finally beheaded, she exudes milk rather than blood, and her body is carried off by angels for burial on Mount Sinai. In the later Middle Ages Catherine became still more explicitly the bride of Christ: extra episodes were added to her legend in which Catherine is persuaded and converted by the greatest of suitors, Christ himself. She becomes his spouse and mystically weds him. Often she is shown in later medieval paintings accepting a nuptial ring from the infant Christ as he sits on the Virgin's lap.

Her most frequent attributes are the palm and sword of virgin martyrdom, and the spiked wheel devised for her torture. But she is also portrayed with the ring of her mystic marriage to Christ, with the turbaned head of the Emperor Maxentius at her feet and with a book for her learning and a crown for her royalty. Women of royal and noble birth often chose her as their patron saint, but she was important over a wide social and occupational range. Her betrothal to Christ made her the patroness of young unmarried women, and she is also specially associated with nuns (who, when they take their vows, are consecrated to Christ with a ring and a veil). Because of her learning and her victory in debate, she was patron of theologians, philosophers, clerks, students and schoolchildren. Wheelwrights, millers, carters, potters, knife-grinders and other trades using wheels took her as patron, and her miraculous bleeding of milk made her the patron saint of wet-nurses. Considered to be a powerful advocate, she was an intercessor for the dying, and the patron of notaries. She could also intercede for good weather and harvests and for help against ill-fortune and pestilence. She is invoked for diseases of the tongue. She figures on the seal of the Sorbonne and was patroness of Venice, the West's gateway to the East.

The figure of Catherine may owe something to that of the Alexandrian mathematician and philosopher Hypatia. Daughter of a mathematician and a rare example of celibacy among non-Christian women, Hypatia lectured on Plato and Aristotle and perhaps wrote on mathematics in Alexandria until AD 415, when, amidst high religious and political tension in Alexandria, she was lynched by a Christian mob.[24] Several scholars have thought it possible that the Catherine legend originated as a riposte, counterposing to the story of Hypatia a learned Christian woman and her rebuttal of pagan philosophy.[25] The Hypatia story is attractive as an antecedent, but there is a considerable lapse of time between Hypatia's death and the earliest extant Greek accounts of 'Aikaterina', none of which is securely dated before the ninth century. As an embodiment of Christian wisdom and fidelity, Catherine is in any case a figure perennially re-invented by many generations of clerics and scholars.

The first extant Latin texts of Catherine's passion date from the eleventh century, when her cult was further developed in the West. According to an account written by a monk of Saint-Trinité-du-Mont in Rouen between 1054 and 1090, Symeon, a monk of Mount Sinai, brought bone particles and oil from St Catherine's shrine to Rouen in about 1030, the year in which the abbey of Saint-Trinité was founded by Joscelin d'Arques and his wife Emmeline.[26] Since there is no record of Catherine's shrine before European pilgrims and crusaders sought it out in the Third Crusade (begun 1189), the cult may well have been transmitted from Rouen to Sinai rather than the other way round.[27] At all events, Catherine relics were known in Rouen by the late eleventh century, and the abbey itself soon became known as the abbey of the Holy Trinity and of St Catherine. A life of the saint by Ainard of Rouen is lost, but an anonymous account, now known, because of its prolific survival all over medieval Europe, as the 'Vulgate' *Passion*, because of its prolific survival all over medieval Europe, includes among a hundred and more extant manuscripts a number from the late eleventh and the twelfth centuries.[28]

In Britain, William the Conqueror granted Saint-Catherine-de-Mont a sub-priory at Harmondsworth. Though there are a few scattered indications of earlier knowledge of the saint, Catherine's cult began its full development in Britain with the Norman Conquest. It was in part bound up with the development of St Nicholas's cult. Both these saints were important to the Normans, and both had the special ability of exuding precious curative fluids from their bodies and tombs.[29] By the late eleventh century there is a record from Dunstable of an early miracle play associated with Catherine, probably directed by a cleric and performed by schoolboys.[30] In the twelfth century, versions of the saint's passion multiplied and were translated into Anglo-Norman, amongst other vernaculars.[31] By the early thirteenth century, a Middle English Life was in circulation, and a fresco cycle had been painted in the chapel of the Holy Sepulchre, Winchester.[32] Other visual images followed, both in cycles and in single figure paintings, and Catherine also became an increasingly frequent subject of illustration in psalters and books of hours. In later medieval illuminations she is often paired with St Margaret, and in thirteenth-century works with St Lawrence. Catherine remained an important figure both for churchmen and women and for laypeople. At the wedding of Prince Arthur with Katherine of Aragon in 1501, the princess was greeted on her entry into London by 'a faire yonge lady with a wheel in hir hand in liknes of Seint Kateryne, with right many virgyns in every side of her', and bidden to love 'Crist your first make [mate]' and then Arthur, her 'secunde spouse trewe' (an injunction which was lived out in practice by the fifteenth-century holy woman and devotee of Catherine, Margery Kempe, mentioned above).[33]

Latin offices and plays about Catherine were composed for male monastic houses, and she was soon associated with the nascent, exclusively male universities of the twelfth and thirteenth centuries. However, the Latin tradition of Catherine's legend included from at least the twelfth century an address by the saint to well-born women, 'matrons and virgins'. In the legend's sub-plot, the pagan empress is converted by Catherine so that the life shows a 'matron' imitating and following a virgin. In Britain Catherine seems to have been early associated with women. The earliest known record of her in Britain is in a late tenth-century psalter from the Benedictine nunnery of Shaftesbury.[34] Catherine is probably also the 'Caterina' mentioned in Goscelin's late eleventh-century *Book of Encouragement* (*Liber confortatorius*), written for Eve, formerly of the nunnery of Wilton and subsequently a recluse at Angers.[35] Other prayers and hymns to the saint in Anglo-Norman and English, and an early dramatic version of her life in Anglo-Norman, occur in nunnery manuscripts of the thirteenth and later centuries, whilst the earliest Middle English life of the saint was made for women recluses in the early thirteenth century and appears in several manuscript collections of texts for anchoritic and conventual female communities.[36]

Some of the earliest manuscript illustrations of the saint are to be found in thirteenth-century devotional books made for women.[37] Later vernacular versions in Britain are also often associated with women as patrons and dedicatees, while on the Continent Catherine was used as a precedent by many holy women of the thirteenth century and later. Fittingly, Catherine gives her name to the fourteenth-century Dominican tertiary, prophet, counsellor and composer of orally dictated dialogues, Catherine of Siena. This later Catherine is the first woman doctor of the church, declared as such in 1970.

The Life of St Catherine: *author, date and manuscripts*
Clemence of Barking's Anglo-Norman life of St Catherine of Alexandria is one of the earliest vernacular lives of the saint. It survives in three manuscripts, and an extract from it appears in a fourth. The oldest manuscript, Paris, Bibliothèque Nationale, MS nouv. acq. fr. 4503, is from around 1200, and this supports a late twelfth-century date of composition for the life. A second, more securely datable, vernacular life from Barking is extant: the *Life of Edward the Confessor*, in many respects linguistically and stylistically close to the life of St Catherine, was also written

in the late twelfth century, between 1163 and 1189. This too
lends support to a late twelfth-century dating for *Catherine*.
Edward is the work of an anonymous nun of Barking who
claims to be not worthy, or not yet worthy, of being named in
the life of the virgin king. It is possible, though not proven, that
Clemence and the anonymous Barking hagiographer are one
and the same person.[38]

The manuscript evidence suggests a certain contemporary
esteem for Clemence's *Life of St Catherine*. In the earliest manuscript it appears together with the *Life of St Alexis* and the
Voyage of St Brendan, a saint's life framed as a travel romance
and dedicated to Henry I's queen (either to his first wife, Matilda,
or to his second wife, Adeliza). *Catherine* was also copied into
the late thirteenth-century portion of a major collection of lives
used for refectory reading in the nunnery of Campsey Abbey
(now London, British Library, MS Additional 70513, formerly
Welbeck IC1). The life also appears in a collection of saints' lives
made in the second half of the thirteenth century, Paris, Bibliothèque Nationale, MS f. fr. 23112. The text of the life in this
manuscript is extensively adapted into the Picard forms of continental French. In addition, a quotation of twelve lines from the
life appears in a large late thirteenth-century preacher's miscellany (Cambridge, Trinity College, MS B.14.39), suggesting further insular transmission and diffusion of the life.[39] None of these
manuscripts is a direct copy of any of the others. Since some
Anglo-Norman saints' lives survive only in one or two manuscripts, this suggests a relatively large circulation for the life.

Provenance and milieu
At the conclusion of the *Life of St Catherine*, the author names
herself as Clemence, nun of Barking:

> Jo ki sa vie ai translatee
> Par nun sui Clemence numee.
> De Berkinge sui nunain.
> Pur s'amur pris cest oevre en mein. (vv. 2689-92)

(I who have translated her life am called Clemence by name. I am a
nun of [the abbey of] Barking, for love of which I took this work in
hand.)

Though this is the only biographical evidence we have for Clemence, a good deal is known of the nunnery in which she produced her life of the patron saint of female learning, a life written, by Clemence's own account, for love of her abbey. Given the nature and history of the abbey, it is not entirely surprising that either *Catherine* or the anonymous *Edward the Confessor* (see pp. xxiii–xxiv above), both early and accomplished vernacular lives, should have been produced there.[40]

The history of Barking stretches from its seventh-century foundation to the dissolution of the monasteries in the sixteenth century, and the abbey has some claim to be the home of the longest-lived tradition of female learning and literacy in British history. It is useful to consider the milieu offered by such a convent, one of the few nunneries of abbatial rank in post-Conquest Britain. An abbey of Barking's size and status required a large administrative staff for its estates and revenues and had a complex internal social organization. The abbess had a staff of male clerics and lay advisers, stewards and bailiffs: in addition to choir nuns literate enough to perform the offices, the nunnery also required the services of priests and spiritual directors. Such an institution offered opportunities even greater than those of large secular estates for women to work as administrators, managers, landholders, artistic patrons and builders. We can note that the thirteenth-century abbesses' rebuilding of Barking's church created a building bigger than Rochester Cathedral.[41] Given the requirements of the liturgical offices and ceremonies, abbesses and choir nuns also had opportunities as artistic performers and directors. Katherine de Sutton, abbess 1363–76, designed an innovative version of a semi-liturgical Latin Easter play and procession of the cross 'to dispel completely the sluggish indifference of the faithful'.[42] Such occasions were not only grand or solemn: the performances in Barking's church extended to *puerilia solemnia* – festivals of misrule in which a girl abbess was elected for a day, and which were associated with Catherine's and other major saints' feasts.[43]

Socially a large abbey was as varied a miniature world as that of any baronial estate. In an aristocratic and relatively wealthy community of nuns, not all inmates would be consecrated virgins or professed religious, and not all would be permanent inhabitants: nunneries often educated young aristocratic women before marriage, as well as housing separated, divorced, abandoned or widowed women. Barking was used in this way by the Norman and Angevin royal families: Matilda, the first wife of Henry I, became its abbess, as did Matilda, Stephen's queen (and foundress, in 1148, of the church and hospital of St Catherine, which has given its name to St Catherine's Docks in London). Henry II gave the position to Mary, sister of Thomas Becket, in reparation for the murder of the archbishop in 1170, and she was succeeded by Henry's own daughter, Maud.

Barking's royal and noble connections linked it to a wider world in the court and among the aristocracy. Clemence says, as noted above, that the *Life of St Catherine* was written for Barking, but the narrative also addresses 'lords' (*segnurs*, v. 1159). This term occurs in a number of texts and manuscripts belonging to women in Anglo-Norman Britain and may simply function as an inclusive address. But in a text written by a female religious it suggests that mixed audiences, and audiences outside Barking, were also expected to hear the life. The manuscript evidence (see p. xxiv above) suggests that this is exactly what happened. At the dissolution, neither Barking's traditional royal associations nor Jasper and Edmund Tudor's schooling there saved it from being plundered for stone for Henry VIII's palace at Greenwich. But Barking was for some centuries – especially in the twelfth – one of the most cultivated and interesting milieux available to women who were free of, or in respite from, child-bearing and marital duties.

The earliest evidence of learning among the women of Barking dates from the seventh century, when Aldhelm of Malmesbury dedicated his ornate Latin verse-and-prose treatise on the martyrdoms of male and female virgin saints to Abbess Hildelith and her nuns. Aldhelm complimented the women of Barking on their scholarship and the 'rich verbal eloquence' of their letters to him.[44] Until the eleventh century, the principal female biography associated with the abbey was the life of its first abbess, St Ethelburga, which Bede included in his influential history of the English church.[45] In the late eleventh century, the Flemish cleric Goscelin of Saint-Bertin was commissioned to rewrite the

biographies of Barking's saintly abbesses, together with accounts
of the translation of their bodies to new shrines (probably for
the major building programme undertaken by Abbess Ælf-
giva).[46] As well as re-writing and updating extant Latin lives,
Goscelin spent some time interviewing an elderly nun for
information about the earlier abbesses. In the mid-twelfth
century, learned, elaborate and courtly letters in Latin by Osbert
of Clare, prior of Westminster, were sent to Abbess Adeliza and
to Osbert's nieces, who were nuns at Barking.[47] The Latinity of
noble women religious, as of royal women, seems to have been
greater in the first few generations after the Conquest than it
later became. From the late twelfth century, vernacular literary
evidence, such as a collection of the Virgin Mary's miracles in
Anglo-Norman dedicated to 'Dame Mahaut' (probably the
abbess of Barking), increasingly joins the witnesses to Barking's
Latin literacy.[48]

The writing (though not the commissioning) of sacred and
exemplary biography by women appears to be unprecedented in
Britain until the Barking lives of the twelfth century. The production of saints' lives in Anglo-Norman, the *lingua franca* and the
literary language of the post-Conquest ruling classes, was increas-
ing at this period, and an abbey with Barking's traditions and
resources was a propitious environment. Mary Becket, abbess of
Barking, was thanked for the gift of a palfrey by Guernes de
Pont-Sainte-Maxence, who visited Barking in the course of revis-
ing his late twelfth-century life of her brother Thomas Becket.
Guernes mentions 'all the lives composed about the martyr, by
clerics or laypeople, monks or a woman'.[49] Whether or not a lost
life of Becket by a woman is referred to here, Guernes seems
either to have been aware, or to have wished to imply, that he
had female contemporaries capable of writing one. Perhaps his
contact with Barking as a visiting vernacular hagiographer in the
1170s suggested some possibilities to the gifted woman or
women in Barking to whom we owe the *Life of Edward the
Confessor* and the *Life of St Catherine*.

Sources and influences

Clemence of Barking's life follows the long *Vulgate* Latin version
of St Catherine's legend. This, the most widely diffused of the

Latin versions, circulated from the late eleventh or early twelfth century in a longer and in several shorter forms. No text of it survives among the extant medieval books known to have belonged to Barking.[50] Clemence makes more extensive additions than could be accounted for by variations between extant manuscripts of the Latin text and the particular copy of it which she used. Further work needs to be done on Clemence's sources before a full picture of her reading and her learning is possible, though it is clear that she knew, and made skilful use of, courtly, devotional and didactic literary registers, in both Latin and Anglo-Norman. The *Vulgate* life of Catherine is written in a fairly elaborate Latin, generally handled with skill and assurance in the translation. Works by St Anselm and perhaps also by Honorius of Autun, together with knowledge of the liturgy, of vernacular courtly and devotional lyric and narrative, and of 'wisdom' and homiletic registers, contribute to the transformation and development of the Latin source.[51]

The Anglo-Norman text follows the order of events in the Latin *Vulgate*, but the themes of the many speeches of the saint and the pagans are often extended or altered. A distinct narrating voice and stance is created, within which the events and speeches of the Latin source are embedded and through which ethical and moral reflection and comment are added. Sentential and proverbial texts were a highly valued part of Anglo-Norman literary culture. Latin and vernacular versions of Cato's *Distichs* and other proverbial collections circulated, as did debate poetry. Marie de France's *Fables* and a vernacular translation of exegesis on the biblical book of Proverbs (probably commissioned by Lady Aëliz de Cundé) suggest that women were interested in this material.[52] The verses from Clemence's *Catherine* excerpted in the Trinity manuscript's preaching collection mentioned above (p. xxiv) consist of proverbial reflection.

Clemence refers in her prologue (vv. 35–46) to a previous vernacular version, which she says is in need of improvement if it is to remain efficacious in a world growing older and 'more envious' (vv. 37–8).[53] It is possible that this earlier vernacular life was the dramatic version of the legend represented by a fragmentary Anglo-Norman text in the John Rylands University Library, Manchester (MS Rylands 6). Some half-dozen lines can be paralleled between the two texts, but in general the fragmentary condition of the Rylands text and the fact that the Latin *Vulgate* is followed relatively closely with respect to narrative order and event make it difficult to see clearly how Clemence used this text or to be absolutely certain that she did use it.[54]

Since Marie de France's prologue to her *Lais* and Clemence's prologue to the *Life of St Catherine* have many points in common, some influence or borrowing may have occurred, but the canon and dating of each woman's *oeuvre* is currently too uncertain for the direction of possible influence to be clear.

Treatment

Confrontations between virgin saints and pagan tyrants can sometimes be heightened and stylized in saints' lives to the extent of becoming a comic-strip battle between good and evil, God and the devil, saint and torturer. In Clemence's version, this conflict is, among other things, an account, written by a learned twelfth-century woman, of the defeat by a solitary woman of recognizably medieval clerics and academic rhetoricians. The saint uses the clerks' own weapons of rhetoric and logic, and she is, as she herself points out at the start of the debate, a woman without access to the emperor's structures of reward and promotion (vv. 645–52). As Simon Gaunt has argued, the contest is on one level a confrontation between a woman's faith and men's learning, while on another Clemence's Catherine portrays the superiority of a woman in the very arts that are argued to be worthless without faith.[55] Composed in, and in the first instance for, a female community, this is an important and challenging account of medieval mappings of learning, gender and spirituality.

The poise and complexity of Clemence's writing are particularly evident in her use of comedy. When Maxentius proposes to make a golden statue in Catherine's honour, the saint's response deftly satirizes Maxentius' gods, his desire for the saint herself, and in general the placing of women on pedestals as forms of idolatry. The emperor asserts that everyone will have to bow down to the statue. But Catherine demurely asks what he proposes to do about perching birds and passing dogs and the activities by which *they* are likely to salute it (vv. 1343–9). Yet there is a theologically serious point at issue here: Maxentius does not have supreme control over all creation, and statues of women are not proper objects of worship when there is a Creator God.

The formal debate staged between Catherine and the emperor's clerks combines comedy and theology with a surprising emotional range. Debate is a particularly characteristic social practice and literary mode in the twelfth century; cathedral schools and the new universities offered courses in rhetoric, logic and formal disputation. Clemence retains the lengthy arguments in her Latin source, and she also adds to them with great effect. Several other Latin and vernacular lives of St Catherine omit the arguments of the debate and simply state that victory went to the saint. Clemence makes the pagan clerks comically arrogant at the outset, but she also treats pagan doctrines and arguments not as stereotyped devilry but as a form of human benightedness. The pagans' positions, whilst wrong, are made comprehensible as positions held by people without the grace of revelation. Even the Emperor Maxentius is allowed to display something of the internal coherence which his faith has for him. He sees Christianity as illogical and cruel in putting its God and its followers to death, whereas his own faith seems natural as well as time-honoured: 'What land is so remote that [its people] do not worship the sun?', he asks (vv. 252–3).

The clerks, moreover, ask questions which Christians might well ask – how *can* God be both god and man? Can death really be redeemed? What need had God, who can save all from death, to die himself? In the late twelfth century such questions were indeed being debated by Christian thinkers in new ways. In particular, the devotional and theological work of Anselm of Canterbury (d. 1109) had begun to shift thought about human salvation from an emphasis on God's victory over the devil to Christ's human incarnation as the means of redeeming humanity.[56] Informed by these issues of doctrine and devotion, and treated in verse at once lyrical and dramatic, Catherine's very full answers and the conversion of her opponents are unexpectedly moving. Death *can* be defeated, resurrection *can* be hoped for: as the leading clerk recognizes, 'It is no small thing that this lady advances' (vv. 1093–4).

Catherine points out that God chose to mediate justice through love, but could have saved the world by the sheer exercise of power or will, had he so chosen (vv. 1001–2). Power, the will and their disposition are important concerns throughout the text. In additions without precedent in the Latin legend, the emperor is shown to be the captive of his impulse: in his initial edict of persecution, the narrative comments on him as an example of those who, since they possess the power to enact their own evil thoughts, are unable to restrain themselves from so doing (vv. 68–74). As Catherine argues, in his idol-worship the emperor inverts proper feudal hierarchies of power by elevating the created over the creator (vv. 284–92). Subsequently, in a speech mourning his own decision to execute his wife, he laments the conflict between his will and his power (vv. 2165–2256). When Porphiry, the captain of the Emperor's guard and his best friend, ignores the command to leave the queen's body unburied, Maxentius laments that all he can now enact is his desire for vengeance and not his desire to have his friend as a comfort and support in his life (vv. 2388–2430). Like most hagiographic tyrants, Maxentius becomes increasingly crazed and ferocious, and his later speeches show his world unravelling in the improper relations of his will and power: 'I am a serf and no emperor', he cries despairingly (v. 2390). This strand of Clemence's narrative can be thought of in part as an anti-*Tristan*: as several critics have noticed, Clemence pointedly echoes this famous story of unregulated passion in Maxentius' lamentation for the wife he is about to kill.[57]

In contrast to this capricious and destructive operation of human will, the figure of Catherine provides a model of committed human volition – of what the twentieth century has called courtly love, and what the Middle Ages knew as *fin'amor*, refined love (a term which probably makes its earliest British appearance in the saints' lives written at Barking).[58] The notion of a permanent disposition of the individual will towards an appropriate and worthy love has been much studied in the context of secular romance, and is associated with figures like Lancelot and Troilus. For the Middle Ages, however, the spiritual registers of the term offer still more opportunity for expressing and analysing love, whilst saints' lives provide a generic opportunity greater than that of secular romance for representing displays of constancy by women. Catherine's love for Christ, unlike Maxentius' uneasy and unstable alliances of will and power, is steady, reciprocal and permanent. Catherine is both model and mediatrix for the mutual love of creator and created, lover and beloved, as the narrative creates a feudal, courtly and spiritual relationship between God and the audience (vv. 2658–88). Catherine is presented from the beginning as God's lover and as a supremely courtly one: she is of noble heart and birth; her love pact with Christ is filled with courtly joy, honour, comfort, sweetness and mutual desire, and it is indissoluble (vv. 31, 147–68, 1357–70). Like the best of modern romance heroes, and in accordance with some important medieval devotional traditions, Christ is not merely a devoted lover. He shows maternal care for Catherine, visiting, healing and feeding her in her dungeon (vv. 1837–62).[59]

Clemence's prologue, like her epilogue, emphasizes the inexhaustible and universal quality of God's goodness (bunté, vv. 9, 2654, 2676, 2685; bien, vv. 11, 14, 16), which never fails those who desire him. St Bernard of Clairvaux, in his influential contemporary treatise on the love of God, argued that God was the only object of desire capable of sustaining and never frustrating the desiring will: St Augustine and St Anselm both asked how God's inexhaustible love can be contained in finite human vessels.[60] For Clemence, as Catherine Batt has argued, the properly disposed human will (bon vuleir, 'good will', vv. 521–2, 2647–50) 'allows God's grace to supplement the gap between our volition and our power'. Indeed, only in love for God 'do social forms find their moral and spiritual value'.[61]

The narrator's own activity in the Life of St Catherine is founded on the desire to will and to do what is good, as far as it lies within one's power (vv. 5–6). In the prologue, this 'good' is defined as the mediation of the story of a true lover of God, as Catherine is called (v. 31). This ethical intention is carried out not just in the work of translation itself, but in the creation of a narratorial presence, which frames and positions narrative events and protagonists, and provides a medium of commentary and discussion in which the text's audience is implicitly engaged. Clemence also elaborates several crowd scenes in which the divergent responses of a whole society are presented in miniature (see vv. 106–28, 1012–52, 2337–52, 2513–28). Her narrative is aware of multiple perspectives, and has some interest in the range of people to whom, as the prologue claims, Christ's goodness is a common source of nourishment and spiritual productivity (vv. 11–14).[62] Clemence's narratorial comments have sometimes been dismissed as a kind of reflex medieval sententiousness, but they are intrinsic to her treatment of the legend. In her version, debate, torture and execution take place not in a fantasy world of spectacle (apart from that inhabited in increasingly crazed isolation by Maxentius), but in a society.

When, for instance, Clemence's Catherine enters Maxentius' hall for the debate, all are astonished by her beauty and she is the object of all eyes. But she is also the subject of a narratorial discussion of the relation between inner disposition and outward demeanour (vv. 595–626). The deportment of the body was a matter of great importance, both in secular courtly milieux and in the training and conduct of professed religious. Prayer manuals and psalters prescribed gestures and postures: contemporary holy men and women were observed keenly and respectfully for manifestations of the sacred in their demeanour and the life of their body.[63] Clemence's Catherine is observed on these rather than on more voyeuristic terms. Unlike some other virgin martyrs, her Catherine is never shown simply as a stripped, naked, female body. A similar concern and respect is shown for the bodies of the converted clerks. One of the longest narratorial comments concerns their miraculous integrity and unblemished preservation in the flames in which Maxentius has them martyred (vv. 1171–1238). Their wholeness is celebrated as a sign of God's goodness (bunté, v. 1190). Their souls may be fed in heaven (v. 1185), but the condition of their bodies on earth is still an important sign and reassurance of the resurrection's power to overcome even the pulverization of death by fire. What may seem an irrelevant piece of good manners on God's part – honouring the clerks by allowing their bodies to remain whole in death – attests the importance of the relation between bodily and spiritual decorum.

The most graphic moment of bodily dismemberment in the legend is therefore all the more striking. The converted queen's breasts, 'which were very beautiful and tender' (v. 2306), are torn off with iron hooks at her husband's command. Maxentius treats the queen as a subversive embodiment of his rule (vv. 2219–42). In his 'new torments' (v. 2253) for her, he destroys her capacity to nurture his lineage. Both as a married man and as a ruler, Maxentius frenziedly attacks his wife and himself: in so far as the authority of a husband and an emperor is invested in the body of a queen, Maxentius here destroys the coherence of his regime. Still more important, however, is the relation between the queen and Catherine. The sub-plot of the queen's martyrdom shows the virgin saint providing a role model for the married woman. The Latin legend implicitly configures virgins, matrons and clerical men in an allegiance against secular power. In Clemence of Barking's version, Catherine's redirection of the queen towards a better lover, a better kingdom, and an eternal rather than a transitory happiness is, as MacBain argues, made more emphatically and strikingly than in any other French vernacular treatment of the legend.[64] The connections here are underlined by a kind of metaphorical transference between the bodies of the queen and of Catherine. One woman loses her breasts, and the other, at her own beheading, bleeds milk. This link between the queen's breasts and Catherine's spiritual fecundity is especially strong according to medieval theories of physiology, which view breast milk as a specialized form of blood. Catherine's own body, with its healing and nourishing fluids of milk and oil, incorporates a death-defeating fertility which transcends even that of the queen consort.

Not only does Catherine offer spiritual fecundity in place of that continual bearing of offspring which was so powerful a factor in medieval women's lives and deaths. She is also consistently eloquent and intelligent: no merely charismatic vessel of the Holy Spirit, Clemence's Catherine remains in possession of her intelligence and is seen to trust and to use it (v. 193). She defeats the philosophers as a superior dialectician as well as someone whose faith gives her speech the efficacy of the Word (vv. 1101–8). Recent studies of the spiritual directors, confessors and correspondents of medieval holy women point to the admiration often felt by these male writers for the women in their pastoral care: such women were sometimes seen as having greater capacities for expressing faith than their academically trained spiritual directors precisely because they were perceived as less rational and hence more closely allied to the humanity of Christ.[65] This perception allocates affective power to individual holy women (and in many historical cases this led to socio-economic power). However, it can also be seen as an intellectual and theological version of the 'angel-in-the-house' or 'Muse' construction of women, another way of putting them on an emotional pedestal.

In the case of Clemence of Barking's Catherine, a learned medieval woman gives an eloquent account of Christian faith which does not require women to be seen as *merely* intuitive and affective or *merely* flesh in their special empathy with Christ in his humanity.[66] Catherine's arguments and Clemence's narratorial mediation unite emotion, intellect, reason and passion in an unusually full and fine exploration of the possibilities of medieval exemplary female biography.

The Life of St Lawrence

St Lawrence

Many elements of Lawrence's legend are apocryphal, but there is a historical basis for his existence. His feast-day of 10 August is still celebrated in the calendar of saints. Lawrence, archdeacon of Rome, was martyred a few days after Pope Sixtus II in AD 258. In the early church, seven deacons, modelled on the seven 'men of honest report, full of the Holy Spirit' of Acts 6:3, helped the priest with the administration of the sacraments and the parish. They were responsible for almsgiving and the care of widows and orphans.[67] Lawrence became one of the most important Roman martyrs and patron saints of the city, with which he was strongly identified. In the twelfth-century pilgrim guide, *The Marvels of Rome*, for example, the sites of Lawrence's interrogation and torture, and the locations of his relics, form one of the most prominent strands of information.

Lawrence's cult was early and widely known throughout Europe. The principal narrative of his martyrdom circulated as part of the Roman Legendary's *Passion of Polychronius* ...

Sixtus, Lawrence and Other Saints. This was a compilation of perhaps the sixth century or earlier, extant in manuscripts from the tenth century.[68] In this *Passion*, Sixtus, Lawrence and other churchmen are unhistorically shown as martyred by Decius Caesar. It was in fact the emperor Valerian (AD 253–60), said in the *Passion* to be Decius' provost, who in AD 258 ordered the persecution in which Sixtus, the bishop of Rome, and his deacons perished.[69] Since Valerian's edict did not specify interrogation but, rather, immediate execution of Christian clerics, much of the narrative of Lawrence's imprisonment and torture is apocryphal, even though Lawrence himself is a historical figure. In the *Passion*, Sixtus, aware that his own arrest and execution are imminent, entrusts the treasure of the church to Lawrence. Lawrence spends it on food and clothes for the poor of Rome, and when Valerian and Decius demand that he surrender it to them he presents the poor people as the church's treasure. Decius has Lawrence extensively tortured, in an effort to make him acknowledge the pagan gods. As Lawrence remains steadfast, he finally has him roasted to death on a gridiron. Lawrence's most distinctive attribute is thus, like Catherine's, an un-Roman form of torture (the gridiron is probably calqued on the martyrdom of another deacon, St Vincent of Saragossa in Spain). Lawrence is represented as cheerfully enduring this hideous slow death and he became celebrated as an example of constancy and fortitude. The antiphon for his feast-day quotes one of his dying speeches: 'On the gridiron, I did not deny you, O God, and touched with fire, O Christ, I acknowledged you.'[70] Even better known are his final words to Decius: *Assum est, versa et manduca* ('It [this side] is roasted, turn me over and eat').[71] Quotations of this speech antedate the *Passion*, the earliest known citation being that of St Ambrose of Milan in the late fourth century. In a letter written in 1913, D. H. Lawrence still thought of 'my dear St Lawrence on his gridiron when he said "Turn me over, brothers, I am done enough on this side" '[72]

Like Catherine, Lawrence was a saint of particular interest to the institutional church, and he also became extremely popular.[73] He is patron of the poor and, since deacons had charge of sacred books, of librarians and booksellers. He is still patron saint of firemen, charcoal burners, glass-blowers, bakers, meat-cooks and ironing-ladies, and he is invoked for the 'fiery' disease of lumbago. In Sicily the falling stars of August are the 'tears of St Lawrence' (tears wept, according to Lawrence's *Passion*, not on the gridiron, but in his earlier work of healing and baptizing). He is portrayed on or with his gridiron and also wearing a deacon's dalmatic. He is seen carrying the Gospels and a processional cross, or a purse or chalice filled with gold pieces.

In medieval Britain, Lawrence's cult was early established. Bede mentions the gift of Lawrence relics from Pope Vitalian to the seventh-century King Oswy of Northumbria.[74] He is mentioned as 'the holy Lawrence who is in Rome' in Ælfric's late tenth-century saints' lives in Old English.[75] In the twelfth century, William of Malmesbury praised Goscelin's eleventh-century life of Lawrence, and Nigel Wireker wrote an elaborate verse Latin passion of Lawrence for the monks of Canterbury.[76] In addition to Lawrence's twelfth-century Anglo-Norman life, Middle English lives were written and continued to circulate and be updated from the thirteenth to the sixteenth century.[77] Many pre-Reformation English churches were dedicated to Lawrence (220 as against Catherine's 57), and he is frequently illustrated in medieval psalters and books of hours. His martyrdom was also dramatized in late medieval saints' plays.[78] He is cited as a counter-example to the simony of contemporary churchmen by Gerald of Wales in the twelfth century and by Langland in the fourteenth century.[79]

As well as retellings of Lawrence's passion, there were many miracle stories featuring chalices and cups, reflecting the perceived power of the eucharistic sacrament, with which Lawrence's role as archdeacon linked him. In his history of the kings of England, written in 1125, William of Malmesbury tells how Henry II, Holy Roman Emperor 1002–24, was cured of a fever by St Lawrence, who appears as 'a young man half-scorched, bearing a golden cup of immense size, full of water' because Henry had restored a church dedicated to the saint and given it a golden chalice.[80] In another story, Henry's unjust suspicion of his wife Cunegund, with whom he had agreed a virgin marriage, is counterbalanced at his death by a golden chalice which he had given to St Lawrence.

Lawrence was also a figure commended to women. Writing to his niece Cecilia in Barking Abbey, Osbert of Clare, prior of

Westminster *c.* 1134, describes for her a recent visionary appearance of St Lawrence in the ancient Roman church of S. Lorenzo
in Veterano. Osbert especially recommends Lawrence to Cecilia
for daily remembrance so that 'in summoning to mind the
triumph of this man in the flames, you extinguish the rising fire
of vices in yourself'.[81] In later years, Barking owned a relic of St
Lawrence.[82] A young woman who developed a special devotion
to Lawrence was an unmarried laywoman probably living in the
parish of St Lawrence, Oxford. She owned the earliest known
English book of hours. This is an exquisite little manuscript of
offices and devotions made in Oxford in the 1240s by William
de Brailes. An extra leaf, apparently added at the express wish
of the book's owner, contains further prayers to the saint and
shows Lawrence's martyrdom on the gridiron with a caption in
French.[83] The de Brailes Hours also illustrates Lawrence's powers
of intercession in its inclusion of the story of a burgess of the
parish of St Lawrence. His almsgiving does not weigh heavily
enough in the scales as angels and devils contend for his soul.
However, over and above his duty of support for the parish church,
the townsman had given a large golden chalice to St Lawrence's
church and in recognition of this the saint adds a chalice which
tips the scales so that the burgess is carried to heaven.[84]

The Anglo-Norman Life of St Lawrence: *date and manuscripts*
The composer of the *Life of St Lawrence* remains anonymous,
but the commissioner of the translation is identified as a
'handmaiden of St Lawrence, who wants the story of Lawrence
and his passion in order to retain him in her memory and to
take his deeds as an example' (vv. 75–9), and who has accord-
ingly requested the vernacular text. Among the nunneries dedicated to the saint, Polesworth in Warwickshire has been
suggested as the home of the recipient of the *Life of St Lawrence*,
though it is also possible that, like the owner of the de Brailes
hours mentioned above, she may have been a laywoman with a
special dedication to, or association with, the saint.[85] Whether
the writer was an inhabitant of a female community dedicated
to St Lawrence, or perhaps the male spiritual director of such a
community, remains unknown. There is no internal evidence in
the life to confirm or to exclude authorship of either gender. The

prologue opens with an invocation to the writer's 'master' (v. 1) for help with deficiencies in the writing (v. 16) and this would fit a monastic or clerical writer addressing a superior or older brother, or a nun addressing her spiritual director. Like the *Life of Catherine*, linguistic and manuscript evidence suggests a date for the Anglo-Norman *Life of Lawrence* not earlier than the late twelfth century, perhaps about 1170. The text is extant in two related late thirteenth-century manuscripts: Paris, Bibliothèque Nationale, MS f. fr. 19525, and London, British Library, MS Egerton 2710. Both manuscripts were written in England, and both comprise extensive collections of saints' lives, biblical and apocryphal narratives, treatises, sermons and lyrics. *Lawrence*'s modern editor concluded that neither manuscript's text was a direct copy of the other, and that both were copies of a common source. The Egerton manuscript was owned by the nuns of Derby Priory at the end of the fifteenth century.[86]

Sources

The Anglo-Norman text's principal source is the story of Sixtus and his deacons as found in the *Passion of St Polychronius . . . Sixtus, Lawrence and Other Saints*, which dates from the late fifth or early sixth century.[87] This Latin *Passion* circulated in pre- and post-Conquest manuscripts, in both full and abridged versions. The *Passion* is the narrative of a group of martyrs, all interconnected by a common persecutor on the one hand, and their own institutional and personal links on the other. In order to focus on Lawrence, the Anglo-Norman writer omits the initial and final martyrdoms of the *Passion* and either cuts out minor characters or abridges their appearances. The martyrdom of Sixtus is retained as a necessary prelude to that of Lawrence (later thirteenth-century continental French prose versions of the *Passion*, by contrast, relate the two martyrdoms as separate narratives).[88] In this section the Latin source is considerably condensed and rearranged. For Lawrence's own martyrdom, on the other hand, the *Passion*'s order of narrative event has been much more closely followed, though here, as throughout, details seem on occasion to have been taken from one or more of the abridged Latin versions rather than from the *Passion* alone.[89]

The translator adds a prologue and an account of the translation's own genesis. Like Clemence of Barking, he or she seems to have considered vernacular precedents for translation from Latin: the prologue is very close to Philippe de Thaon's introduction to his early twelfth-century poem on the calendar, *Computus*. Both texts include a request for help, as well as proverbial remarks about true friendship being displayed in time of need.[90] In the narrative proper, the translator extensively develops Lawrence's arguments and exposition of Christian doctrine in his debate with Decius. The argument becomes a succinct account of salvation and the history of the redemption, underlined by extensive word-play in a manner similar to that of the debate in *Catherine*. Ethical reflection and commentary are also part of the vernacular narration at large, though in a less developed and more occasional way than in the *Life of St Catherine* (see, for example, vv. 333–53). Throughout the narrative, the Anglo-Norman *Lawrence* also draws particularly on the psalter and perhaps on the liturgical offices concerned with St Lawrence. Most of these echoes and resonances are achieved in Anglo-Norman octosyllabics, but occasionally Latin words and phrases are used.[91] These are not invariably taken from the *Passion*, and some evoke fundamental aspects of devotional life such as the *Pater noster* and the creed. It is tempting to see the presence of this other register in the narrative as due to the author's sense of the kind of Latin used by the handmaiden of St Lawrence for whom the poem is written (v. 76). Psalters and some knowledge of liturgical phrases could be expected to be part of such a woman's devotional life.[92]

Treatment

Lawrence's torture on the gridiron is the most prominent and least historical motif of his passion. It is the nexus of several important themes gathered together in the figure of this saint. Food and eating are especially significant in the *Life of St Lawrence*. The saint declares that Decius' promised torment is food that he desires (*douce viande*, 'sweet meat' or 'sweet food', v. 555). Decius inverts this idea, so that Lawrence's final torture makes the saint himself a piece of roasted flesh. Lawrence, however, turns the gridiron on which he is tortured into an altar, by offering himself on it as a sacrifice to God (v. 847). As we have seen, he also invites Decius to turn him over and to eat from his cooked side (vv. 896–7). This taunt, celebrated from at least the fourth century onwards, was powerful in the context of mutual accusations between early Christians and pagans regarding their religions' food symbolism and practices. In Eusebius' *Ecclesiastical History*, for instance, a young martyr of Lyons is burnt in an iron chair and he remarks that it is not Christians who are cannibals, but the pagans who are roasting him. Another martyr comments that, since Christians will not eat the blood of animals (by making pagan sacrifices), they are unlikely to eat children.[93] Careful distinction of appropriate and inappropriate symbolic values for food is of obvious importance in a religion whose central sacrament is the eating of God's body and blood. These themes retained their force – and their dangers – in the Christian Middle Ages, when, for example, Jews were accused of the ritual murder and eating of children, and stories were told of their conversion on seeing the bleeding Host.[94] In the twelfth century, Gerald of Wales tells a story of bread illegitimately baked on Lawrence's feast-day which was seen to be 'dripping with blood, inside and out'.[95] Lawrence's offer of his roasted flesh to Decius, for all its black comedy, assimilates his passion to Christ's sacrifice. Torture feeds Lawrence's faith, and Decius' torture makes him the food of faith.

Among all the young churchmen persecuted along with Pope Sixtus, Lawrence, as archdeacon, is particularly associated with the Eucharist, since it was his task to assist Sixtus in celebrating Mass (see vv. 225–6). In the early church it was the task of the deacon to present the chalice to the people, but for much of the Middle Ages the chalice was not part of lay communion. A decree forbidding all except those in holy orders to touch the chalice was attributed in medieval tradition to Pope Sixtus. As an archdeacon, Lawrence is thus a figure who controls and displays the sacrament of Christ's blood as well as imitating Christ's sacrifice in his passion. His numerous medieval chalice miracles and his ritual care of the blood of Christ complement his torture on the gridiron.[96]

Lawrence also embodies a further important nexus of Christian meaning in his presentation of the poor of Rome as the church's treasure. This, too, is appropriate to his institutional role (duties of deacons in the early church included informing the bishop about the state of his flock, collecting the offertory at Mass, administering alms and visiting Christians in prison).[97] The gold and silver of chalices is one form of church treasure and as such is sought by Decius, but the church and all its members on earth are also the body of Christ. Feeding the church and caring for the riches of the church are thus potentially identical rather than opposed activities, and the relations between body, blood, treasure and value complement the importance of sacrificed flesh in Lawrence's legend. The link is explicitly made in terms of food: the poor are said to have eaten and drunk the church treasures expended on their behalf by Lawrence (v. 408) and Decius invites Lawrence to have them come and eat the food of torture with him (vv. 561–2).

The major themes of Lawrence's legend are perennially important in medieval Christian culture, but emphases and effects can shift in different treatments. In a later Middle English translation in the *South English Legendary*, Lawrence's 'sweet meat' of torment becomes simply 'merry comfort'.[98] Along with the saint's cheerful heroism, the Anglo-Norman version retains the resonant play on food and sacrifice embodied in Lawrence's legend and, indeed, further develops it in Lawrence's debate with Decius. Here, the fruit of the cross gives eternal life to human flesh (vv. 495, 500–1), and God is the maker who does not need the precious metals of pagan idols for his material (vv. 435, 444–63). This God is identifiable with the humanity of his followers, and shares his nature with the poor who both constitute and consume the church's treasure (vv. 407–8, 418–20). In eleventh- and twelfth-century social theory the poor had a much-discussed role in the economy of salvation: they provided the rich with an opportunity for charity and so became a means for 'the purchase of paradise'.[99] Almsgiving was a regular and important practice among most classes. In Anglo-Norman saints' lives, theories and practices of almsgiving and charity are extensively alluded to and exemplified. The anonymous life of Edward the Confessor by a nun of Barking, for instance, shows the king repeatedly treating the poor as his fellow flesh and blood and healing them through contact with his own body.[100]

The treatment of Lawrence himself in the Anglo-Norman version parallels contemporary devotional practices regarding the body of Christ, which was of particular importance in women's devotional lives. Numerous lyrics, meditations and prayers addressed to or used by women inculcate the contemplation of Christ's crucified body.[101] Christ-like in his passion, and with privileged access to the Eucharist, Lawrence is an appropriate exponent of the sacrificed flesh and the bloody fruit of the redemption. The figure of the saint could be said to be sweet food (vv. 555, 557) for the contemplation of the 'handmaiden of Christ' (v. 76) for whom the life was written. In addition to the symbolic resonances of Lawrence's death on the gridiron, his demeanour during torture provides, like Catherine's, a striking example of the bodily composure celebrated in saints as an outward manifestation of inner spirituality. The figure of this youthful cleric and martyr must have had much to say both to the handmaiden who requested his Anglo-Norman life and to the female communities and other audiences who subsequently owned or heard texts of it.

Style

As noted earlier, saints' lives are largely composed for oral delivery. Not only do they frequently include many speeches by the saint and the persecutor, but passages which may seem merely didactic or expository on the page are often designed for dramatic aural effect. *Catherine* and *Lawrence* include many stylistic effects which are lost in English prose translation, so a brief account of the two texts as Anglo-Norman verse is given here.

In the *Life of St Catherine* the Latin prose source is transformed into elegantly handled Anglo-Norman octosyllabics. These short rhyming couplets were the common currency of a great deal of Anglo-Norman narrative and descriptive writing. The octosyllabic line is normally, but not invariably, divisible into two parts, of which the first usually ends on a stressed (tonic) syllable. This is most frequently the fourth syllable of the line, which is thus divided into two hemistichs. Many of Clemence's lines follow this regular pattern:

Sulunc le tens | bien ordené. (v. 36)

Se nul de vus | le cuntredit
Ja pois n'avrad | de mort respit. (vv. 85–6)

But a high proportion follow other possible variations, with a caesura after the third or fifth syllable:

   1   2   3   4   5   6   7 8
Que par tei | ma moillier perdi. (v. 2476)

   1 2 3 4 5 6 7 8
Plurer e batre | lur peitrines. (v. 2526)

The line of verse is usually the syntactic unit, and full enjambment is rare. The flexibility of the caesura's placing, and the use of various types of end and internal rhyme and assonance, are the chief means of rhythmical and rhetorical variation. Leonine rhyme (where the rhyme includes the consonant preceding the rhyming tonic vowel) is also sometimes used, as in:

Par poesté, nient par na**ture**,
Devint li faitre cria**ture**. (vv. 837–8)

Coment viveras tu **sanz mei**
Et ge coment viverai **sanz tei**? (vv. 2175–6)

Rich rhyme (where the last syllable of the line rhymes with the syllable preceding the caesura) is relatively rare:

E que par **hume** varjast l'**ume**. (v. 999)

A prominent stylistic trait is the use of various figures of repetition. These sometimes follow the Latin source, as in, for example, the saint's declaration of her preference for Christ when the emperor offers to make her his second wife:

Il [Christ] **est mun** los e **ma** honur;
Il est ma glorie e **ma** valur;
Mun delit [est] e **mun** cunfort:
Ma dulçur est e **mun** deport. (vv. 1361–4)

(He is my renown and my honour; he is my glory and my worth. He is my pleasure and my comfort, my sweetness and my delight.)

Here the repetitions follow the Vulgate's 'ille gloria **mea, ille**
generositas **mea,** ille amor **meus,** ille dulcedo et dilectio **mea'**
('He is my glory, my nobility, my love, my sweetness, my
beloved').[102] Equally, there may be rhetorical elaboration without a basis in the Latin source. In the saint's next speech for
instance, we find

> Iço desir, iço demant.
> Bien dei pur lui peine suffrir,
> Quant il deigna pur mei murir
> Si mestiers est, sufferai mort,
> Car pur mei la suffrid a tort. (vv. 1396–1400)

(I desire and request this. I ought to suffer pain readily for him, since
he deigned to die for me. If necessary I shall suffer death, for he did
so undeservedly on my behalf.)

This is based on a speech in the Vulgate: 'dignum est ut et ego
pro eius nomine non solum penas, sed si sic necesse est etiam
mortem, sustineam' ('it is right that I too for his name's sake
endure not only suffering but if necessary even death', 177/
637–8). The Latin text is not the source of the figures used here
to heighten the saint's declaration. They include (in the terminology of classical rhetoric as inherited by the Middle Ages)
paregmenon (repetition of stem with varied inflections, tenses or
parts of speech, as in *suffrir, sufferai, suffrid*; *murir, mort*);
anaphora (repetition of initial words in successive clauses as in
iço ... iço, v. 1396, and repetition with double elements as in
pur mei ... pur mei, vv. 1398, 1400, and with variations, as in
pur lui, v. 1397), alliteration (desir, demant, dei, deigna), assonance (*dei ... peine ... deigna ... mei*). Such choices suggest
some familiarity with Latin stylistics combined with a confident
deployment of the resources of Anglo-Norman octosyllabic
narrative.

Not all the lines in *Catherine* are regular octosyllabics, and a
number of lines have fewer or more than eight syllables. This is
a common feature of Anglo-Norman verse, which is generally,
but not uncontroversially, reckoned to be less regular than
continental French verse. It is usually assumed that the irregularities are scribal. Manuscript evidence often suggests that a

regular octosyllabic line has been lost in transmission, and may be restored from another manuscript. For example, in the oldest extant manuscript (Paris, Bibliothèque Nationale, MS nouv. acq. fr. 4503 (MacBain MS A)), there is a couplet:

> 1 2   3 4   5 6   7 8
> Unkes a nul | ne volt failir.
>
> 1 2 34(?)56(?) 7 8
> Ki de lui | oust desir. (vv. 19–20)

Here the second line either has only six syllables or irregularly splits two diphthongs across separate syllables. It can be restored to a more regular pair of octosyllabic lines by taking the reading of a later manuscript (London, British Library, MS Additional 70513 (MacBain, MS W)):

> 1 2   3 4   5 6   7 8
> Unkes a nul | ne volt failir.
>
> 1 2 3   45   6   7 8
> Ki de lui amer | eit desir.

(where *a|mer* properly forms two syllables).[103]

However, it is very probable that Anglo-Norman verse was increasingly influenced by English accentual (stress-based) metres, and irregularities cannot always be simply assumed to be due to accidents of transmission. In the native English alliterative metres, the number of syllables per line is highly flexible, since it is not the syllabic count but the pattern of stresses that determines the metrical shape of a line. It is at least possible that what appears to be irregularity or scribal careless-ness from the viewpoint of regular continental French versifica-tion may have been an extra resource or authorial flexibility for an Anglo-Norman versifier.[104] It has been plausibly argued that Chaucer continues to be influenced by English accentual verse even in his adoption of French octosyllabics and other appar-ently syllabic lines (such as the decasyllabic 'riding rhyme' of *The Canterbury Tales*).[105] The great flexibility of Chaucer's octosyllabics is perhaps anticipated in Anglo-Norman versifica-tion. Clemence's octosyllabics are certainly supple and accom-plished, embracing a considerable stylistic and thematic range in dramatic, lyrical and expository registers. The redemption is frequently staged as a debate between God and the devil in medieval literature, most famously perhaps in Langland's treatment of the harrowing of hell in Passus XVIII of *Piers Plowman*. In the *Life of St Catherine*, word-play on *fruit*, on *fust* ('wood' – as in the wood of the cross) and *fust/fud* (subjunctive and preterite forms of the verb 'to be') marks a sustainedly lyrical passage of some fifty lines (see vv. 951–1006) in Catherine's argument to the clerks. Here, the very fabric and forms of language seem expressive of the turn in human hopes given by the redemption, and what in pagan terms remains an irresoluble paradox becomes converted into the language of faith:

> N'est tei avis que ço dreit *fust*, [would be]
> Que cil ki venqui *par le fust*, [by the wood]
> Que *par le fust fust* pois vencu, [by the wood, would be]
> Par le *fruit* ki *fud* pois rependu? [fruit, was]
> Se l'Enemi l'ume enginna, [the devil man deceived]
> Qu'il le *fruit del fust* esraça, [fruit, of the wood]
> E l'ume enginna l'Enimi [man deceived devil]
> Par le *fruit* qu'*el fust* rependi. [fruit, on the wood] (vv. 987–94)

> (Do you not think it right that he who conquered by means of
> the tree was then by that same means conquered himself, by
> the fruit which was hung on it once more? If the Enemy
> deceived man so that he tore the fruit from the tree, man then
> deceived the Enemy through the fruit which he hung again on
> the tree.)

Many of the figures already noted appear here, together with *conversio* (repetition of final words) in vv. 987–8, and a form of *anadiplosis* (repetition of the final word of a clause at the beginning of the next) in v. 989. In the chiastic-patterning of individual lines (*Enemi, l'ume, enginna* : *l'ume, enginna, Enimi*, vv. 991, 993) and in the interweaving of the fruit of the cross with the subsidiary theme of guile (vv. 990, 992, 994; 991, 993), the devil's ingenuity in plotting against humanity is itself here seen to have become part of God's redemptive design.

Much of what has been already said about the *Life of St Catherine* applies to the *Life of St Lawrence*. This poem is also written in octosyllabic couplets, with some irregular lines, with a flexible positioning of the medial caesura and with occasional use of rich and of leonine rhyme.[106] *Lawrence*'s densest lexical repetition plays on *fait, faiture* and *creature/creator*, opposing manufacture to creation, human ingenuity to the Word. As in the case of the *Life of St Catherine*, the poem sustains this play in an exhilarating way over long passages. Lawrence's speech (vv. 437–63), with its insistent repetition of the word *fait* ('makes', 'does') for Decius' merely human gods, becomes a kind of lyric taunting: for instance,

> Lorenz dit: 'Ton deu que vei ici
> Est ceo qu'om **fait**, et ne **fait** rien,
> Car il ne **fait** ne mal ne bien.
> Il est **fait** cumme **faiture**.' (vv. 444–7)

(Lawrence said: 'Your god whom I see here is what man
makes, and itself makes nothing, for it does nothing either evil
or good; it is made as a manufactured thing.')

Like the *Life of St Catherine*, the *Life of St Lawrence* also expounds the redemption, interweaving the themes of cross, death, fruit and life, and using rhyme, assonance, *hiatus* and *paregmenon* and other forms of repetition:

> **Mort nos dona** li premiers **fruiz**,
> **Vie nos dona** icist en cruiz;
> Par **fust fusmes** tuit perdu,
> Par **fust** ravun **vie** et salu.
> Cum **cel arbre porta** le **fruit**
> Par unt nos **fusmes** tuit destruit,
> **Icest arbre** le **fruit porta**
> Qui la **vie nos dona**.
> **Cela porta** la **mort** en la pome
> Et cest, **vie** en la char de homme.
> Cil **morut** qui cel **fruit manja**;
> Qui cest **manjue**, si **vivra**. (vv. 494–505)

(The first fruit gave us death: this one, on the cross, gives us life; through the wood [of the tree] we were completely lost, through the wood [of the cross] we gain life and salvation again. As that tree bore the fruit by which we were completely destroyed, so this tree bore the fruit which gave us life. That one carried death in the apple and this one life, in the flesh of a man. He who ate this fruit died: whoever eats this will live.)

As with the *Life of St Catherine*, the power of the saint's speech is heightened by its contrast to that of the tyrant. The pagan speakers do not have the benefit of the puns and homonyms which express the saints' fuller command of language and God's meaning.

It is not always clear why the author retains some Latin words untranslated: the terms for instruments of torture are kept and explained as technical terms as one might expect, but so too are Roman place-names associated with Lawrence's place of burial, and various phrases from prayers and other devotional formulae. As noted earlier, these may indicate the register of Latin and the formulae which the 'handmaiden' of St Lawrence (v. 76) could be expected to recognize.

JOCELYN WOGAN-BROWNE
GLYN S. BURGESS

References

1 On these aspects of saints' cults, see R. C. Finucane, *Miracles and Pilgrims: Popular Beliefs in Medieval England* (London: Dent, 1977); *Saints and their Cults: Studies in Religious Sociology, Folklore and History*, ed. Stephen Wilson, (Cambridge: Cambridge University Press, 1983); and Jonathan Sumption, *Pilgrimage: An Image of Medieval Religion* (Totowa, NJ: Rowman and Littlefield, 1975).

2 See further, J. W. Earle, 'Typology and Iconographic Style in Early Medieval Hagiography', *Studies in the Literary Imagination*, 8 (1975), 15–46.

3 See John Frankis, 'The Social Context of Vernacular Writing in Thirteenth-Century England: The Evidence of the Manuscripts', in *Thirteenth-Century England I: Proceedings of the Newcastle-upon-Tyne Conference, 1985*, ed. P. R. Coss and S. D. Lloyd, (Woodbridge: Boydell, 1986), pp. 175–84.

4 *Ancrene Wisse*, ed. Geoffrey Shepherd (1959; repr. Exeter: University of Exeter Press, 1985), p. 9/24–33; *Anchoritic Spirituality: Ancrene Wisse and Associated Works*, trans. Anne Savage and Nicholas Watson (Mahwah, NJ: Paulist Press, 1991), p. 181.

5 To the 13,000 lines by the writer known to modern audiences as Marie de

France, the three saints' lives certainly by women enable us to add another 14,000 lines. Marie de France is the author of a collection of short narratives about love (*lais*), and she is also probably the same Marie who produced a collection of *Fables*, and perhaps the Marie who wrote a work on St Patrick's Purgatory (*The Lais of Marie de France*, trans. Glyn S. Burgess and Keith Busby (Harmondsworth: Penguin Books, 1986), Introduction, pp. 7–17). On the hagiographic women writers of twelfth- and thirteenth-century Britain, see W. MacBain, 'Anglo-Norman Women Hagiographers', in *Anglo-Norman Anniversary Essays*, ed. Ian Short, ANTS Occasional Publications 2 (London: ANTS, 1993), pp. 235–50; J. Wogan-Browne, '"Clerc u lai, muïne u dame": Women and Anglo-Norman Hagiography in the Twelfth and Thirteenth Centuries', in *Women and Literature in Britain, 1150–1500*, ed. Carol M. Meale (Cambridge: Cambridge University Press, 1993), pp. 61–85, and 'Wreaths of Thyme: *Translatio* and the Female Narrator in Anglo-Norman Hagiography', in *The Medieval Translator* 4, ed. Roger Ellis and Ruth Evans (Exeter: Exeter University Press, 1994), pp. 46–65.

6 The lives are edited in O. Södergaard, *La vie d'Edouard le confesseur: Poème anglo-normand du XIIe siècle* (Uppsala: Almqvist & Wiksell, 1948), and *La vie sainte Audrée: Poème anglo-normand du XIIIe siècle* (Uppsala: Almqvist & Wiksell, 1955). The *Life of Catherine* has 2700 lines, the anonymous *Vie d'Edouard le confesseur* 6685 lines, and the *Vie sainte Audrée* 4620 lines.

7 On canonization rates, see Jane Tibbetts-Schulenberg, 'Sexism and the Celestial Gynaceum – from 500–1200', *Journal of Medieval History*, 4 (1978), 117–33; and André Vauchez, *La Sainteté en occident au moyen âge* (Rome: Ecole française de Rome, 1980).

8 There are traces of a lost life of Ela, countess of Salisbury and thirteenth-century foundress of Laycock Abbey, perhaps written in Latin by her sub-prioress and successor, Beatrice of Kent (see J. C. Russell, *Dictionary of Writers of Thirteenth-Century England*, Bulletin of the Institute of Historical Research, Special Supplement 3 (London: Longman, 1936; repr. 1967), p. 23). Some nuns composed memorial verses for others in the mortuary rolls exchanged between different nunneries. See Leopold Delisle, *Rouleaux des morts du IXe au XVe siècle*, Société de l'Histoire de France (Paris: Renouard, 1866). There are no known vernacular examples of women writing lives of other post-Conquest women. For the Latin life of Christina of Markyate, see *The Life of Christina of Markyate: A Twelfth-Century Recluse*, ed. and trans. C. H. Talbot (Oxford: Clarendon Press, 1959; repr. 1987).

9 See M. T. Clanchy, *From Memory to Written Record: England 1066–1307*, 2nd edn (Oxford: Blackwell, 1993), ch. 7; Joan M. Ferrante, 'The Education of Women in the Middle Ages in Theory, Fact, and Fantasy', in *Beyond their Sex: Learned Women of the European Past*, ed. Patricia H. La Balme (New York and London: New York University Press, 1980), pp. 9–42.

10 On Anglo-Norman literary patronage, see Ian Short, 'Patrons and Polyglots: French Literature in Twelfth-Century England', *Anglo-Norman Studies*, 14

(1992), 229–49. On saints' lives, see Wogan-Browne, 'Women and Anglo-Norman Hagiography' (see 5 above). On women as religious founders, see Sally Thompson, *Women Religious: The Founding of English Nunneries after the Norman Conquest* (Oxford: Clarendon Press, 1992), ch. 9; and Sharon K. Elkins, *Holy Women of Twelfth-Century England* (Chapel Hill, NC: University of North Carolina Press, 1988).

11 See Lois Huneycutt, 'The Idea of the Perfect Princess: The *Life of St Margaret* in the Reign of Matilda II (1100–1118)', *Anglo-Norman Studies*, 12 (1989), 81–97.

12 On Isabella and Richard, bishop of Chichester (1197–1253), see D. Jones, 'The Medieval Lives of Richard of Chichester', *Analecta Bollandiana*, 105 (1987), 105–29. Matthew Paris's life of Edmund of Abingdon, archbishop of Canterbury (1195–1240), is dedicated to Isabella (see A. T. Baker, 'La Vie de saint Edmond, archevêque de Cantorbéry', *Romania*, 55 (1929), 332–81 (pp. 338–40, p. 343, vv. 28–30).

13 See *The Life of Christina of Markyate*, ed. Talbot.

14 See Louis Carolus-Barré, 'Un Nouveau parchemin amulette et la légende de sainte Margeurite patronne des femmes en couches', *Comptes-rendus de l'Académie des Inscriptions et Belles-Lettres* (1979), 256–75; J. Wogan-Browne, 'The Apple's Message: Some Post-Conquest Hagiographic Accounts of Textual Transmission', in *Late Medieval Religious Texts and their Transmission: Essays in Honour of A. I. Doyle*, ed. Alastair Minnis, York Manuscripts Conferences 1991: Proceedings Series 3 (Cambridge: Brewer, 1994), pp. 39–51.

15 On chaste marriage, see Dyan Elliott, *Spiritual Marriage: Sexual Abstinence in Medieval Wedlock* (Princeton, NJ: Princeton University Press, 1993). For some Anglo-Norman examples, see Janice M. Pindar, 'The Intertextuality of Old French Saints' Lives: St Giles, St Evroul and the Marriage of St Alexis', *Parergon*, n.s. 6A (1988), 11–21.

16 Bede, *A History of the English Church and People*, trans. Leo Sherley-Price, rev. R. E. Latham (Harmondsworth: Penguin Books, 1968), bk IV, chs 19–20.

17 For lives of these saints, see the bibliography given in Wogan-Browne, 'Women and Anglo-Norman Hagiography', n. 4.

18 For the life of Elizabeth by Bozon, see *Seven More Poems by Nicholas Bozon*, ed. M. Amelia Klenke, Franciscan Institute Publications Historical Series 2 (New York and Louvain: Franciscan Institute, 1951), pp. 59–74.

19 *The Book of Margery Kempe*, ed. H. E. Allen and S. B. Meech, EETS os 212 (London: Oxford University Press, 1940), bk I, ch. 22, pp. 50–3; trans. Barry Windeatt, *The Book of Margery Kempe* (Harmondsworth: Penguin Books, 1985) pp. 86–8.

20 On modern romance, see Tanya Modleski, *Loving with a Vengeance: Mass-Produced Fantasies for Women* (Hamden, Conn.: Archon, 1982); and Janice A. Radway, *Reading the Romance: Women, Patriarchy, and Popular Literature*

(Chapel Hill, NC: University of North Carolina Press, 1984; repr. London: Verso, 1987). On medieval and modern romance, see *Romance Revisited*, ed. Lynne Pearce and Jackie Stacey (London: Lawrence and Wishart, 1995). On hagiography and modern romance, see J. Wogan-Browne, 'The Virgin's Tale', in *Feminist Readings in Middle English Literature: The Wife of Bath and All her Sect*, ed. L. Johnson and R. Evans (London: Routledge, 1994), pp. 165–94. On saints' lives and rape, see Jane Tibbetts Schulenberg, 'The Heroics of Virginity: Brides of Christ and Sacrificial Mutilation', in *Women in the Middle Ages and the Renaissance: Literary and Historical Perspectives*, ed. Mary Beth Rose (Syracuse, NY: Syracuse University Press, 1986), pp. 29–72; and Kathryn Gravdal, *Ravishing Maidens: Writing Rape in Medieval French Literature and Law* (Philadelphia, Pa: University of Pennsylvania Press, 1991), pp. 21–41.

21 See *Guide for Anchoresses*, part 8, in *Medieval English Prose for Women*, ed. and trans. B. Millett and J. Wogan-Browne (Oxford: Oxford University Press, 1990; repr. 1992), p. 136, lines 13–19.

22 *The Life of Christina of Markyate*, ed. Talbot; Thomas Head, 'The Marriages of Christina of Markyate', *Viator*, 21 (1990), 75–101; J. Wogan-Browne, 'Saints' Lives and the Female Reader', *Forum for Modern Language Studies*, 27 (1991), 314–32.

23 For much of what follows we are indebted to Farmer: L. Réau, *L'Iconographie de l'art chrétien* (Paris: Presses Universitaires de France, 1958), t. III, pt 1, pp. 262–72; G. B. Bronzini, *La leggenda di Santa Caterina d'Alexandria: passioni grechi e latine* (Rome: Accademia Nazionale dei Lincei, 1960); and Jennifer Relvyn Bray, 'The Legend of St Katherine in Later Middle English' (unpublished Ph.D. thesis, University of London, 1984).

24 See J. M. Rist, 'Hypatia', *Phoenix*, 19 (1965), pp. 214–25; and Gillian Clark, *Women in Late Antiquity: Pagan and Christian Life-Styles* (Oxford: Clarendon Press, 1993), section 5.3, 'Philosphic Women' (pp. 130–3).

25 See Bronzini, *La leggenda di Santa Caterina*, p. 296. According to Eusebius' *Ecclesiastical History*, bk VIII, ch. 14, one well-born Christian woman of Alexandria 'overcame the impassioned soul of Maxentius by her strong courage', and though 'renowned for wealth and birth and education, she nevertheless counted all as second to chastity' (trans. R. J. Deferrari, *Eusebius Pamphili: Ecclesiastical History*, The Fathers of the Church 29 (Washington, DC: Catholic University of America Press, 1955; repr. 1969), p. 197. She was, however, dispossessed of her estates and banished, not martyred.

26 See R. Fawtier, 'Les Reliques rouennaises de sainte Catherine d'Alexandrie', *Analecta Bollandiana*, 41 (1923), 357–68 (pp. 358–9).

27 No such shrine is known to ninth-century pilgrims to Mount Sinai. See Bronzini, *La leggenda di Santa Caterina*, pp. 412–15; and C. W. Jones, 'The Norman Cults of Sts. Catherine and Nicholas, saec. xi', in *Hommages à André Boutemy*, ed. Guy Cambier, Collection Latomus 145 (Brussels: Latomus, 1976), pp. 216–30 (esp. pp. 218–19, 229); repr. in C. W. Jones, *Saint Nicholas of*

Myra, Bari, and Manhattan: Biography of a Legend (Chicago and London: University of Chicago Press, 1978), pp. 144–54.

28 Jones, 'Norman Cults', p. 229. The Vulgate text is edited in E. J. Dobson and S. R. T. O. d'Ardenne, *Seinte Katerine*, EETS, ss 7 (Oxford: Oxford University Press, 1981), pp. 144–203.

29 See Jones, 'Norman Cults', pp. 225–6, 229–30.

30 Geoffrey of Le Mans borrowed costumes from St Albans abbey for this performance in Dunstable. When they were lost in a fire, Geoffrey became a monk himself in reparation, eventually becoming abbot of St Albans in 1119. See Jones, *St Nicholas of Bari*, p. 153, and Karl Young, *The Drama of the Medieval Church* (Oxford: Clarendon Press, 1933; repr. 1962), vol. II, p. 308 n. 2, p. 541. In addition to his early connection with Catherine's cult in England Geoffrey is well known for his spiritual friendship with the recluse and foundress Christina of Markyate (see p. xiv above).

31 For other Anglo-Norman and French lives, see E. C. Fawtier-Jones, 'Les Vies de sainte Catherine d'Alexandrie en ancien français', *Romania*, 56 (1930), W. MacBain, 'Five Old French Renderings of the *Passio sancte Katerine virginis*', in *Medieval Translators and their Craft*, ed. Jeanette M. A. Beer, Studies in Medieval Culture 25 (Kalamazoo, Mich.: University of West Michigan, Medieval Institute Publications, 1989), pp. 41–63. For Middle English lives, see C. d'Evelyn, 'Legends of Individual Saints', in *A Manual of the Writings in Middle English*, ed. J. Burke Severs (Hamden, Conn.: Archon Books, 1967–), fasc. 2 (1970), pp. 599–602. On Latin and vernacular versions in Britain, see Bray, 'The Legend of Saint Katherine'.

32 Ethel Carleton Williams, 'Mural Paintings of St Catherine in England', *Journal of the British Archaeological Association*, 3rd ser. 19 (1956), 20–33.

33 *The Receyt of the Ladie Katerine*, ed. Gordon Kipling, EETS, os 296 (Oxford: Oxford University Press for the EETS, 1990), p. 13, lines 33–5, and p. 14, lines 74–5. For Margery Kempe, see *The Book of Margery Kempe*, ed. Allen and Meech, trans. Windeatt.

34 Michael Lapidge, *Anglo-Saxon Litanies of the Saints*, HBS 106 (London: Boydell for the HBS, 1991), pp. 286 and 83.

35 'The *Liber confortatorius* of Goscelin of Saint Bertin', ed. C. H. Talbot, in *Analecta Monastica*, ed. M. M. Lebreton, J. Leclercq, C. H. Talbot, 3e série, Studia Anselmiana, 37 (Rome: Pontifical Institute of St Anselm, 1955), bk IV, p. 115, 1.20. The extant manuscript, London, British Library, MS Sloane 3103, is a late twelfth-century copy and includes a fragmentary hymn to Catherine (see Bray, 'The Legend of St Katherine', p. 52).

36 A thirteenth-century Anglo-Norman account of Catherine's life in the form of a lyric prayer, 'Très duce Katerine', appears in London, British Library, MS Egerton 613, fol. 6ᵛ (almost certainly a nunnery manuscript). See *Recueil d'anciens texts bas-latins, provençaux et français*, ed. P. Meyer (Paris: Vieweg,

1874–7), pp. 375–6. The dramatic version of the life of St Catherine in Manchester, John Rylands University Library, MS French 6, was once part of a manuscript (also including a copy of the *Life of St Lawrence*) owned by the nuns of Derby priory. See D. W. Russell, 'The Manuscript Source of the Fragment, Rylands French MS 6', *Bulletin of the John Rylands Library*, 71 (1989), 41–7. For the manuscripts of the early Middle English *Seinte Katerine*, see *Seinte Katerine*, ed. d'Ardenne and Dobson, pp. xliii–liii; and Savage and Watson, *Anchoritic Spirituality*, pp. 259–84.

37 Clare Donovan, *The de Brailes Hours: Shaping the Book of Hours in Thirteenth-Century Oxford* (London: British Library Publications, 1991), p. 63 (fig. 34, the de Brailes Hours), p. 148 (fig. 94, the Harley Hours).

38 See W. MacBain, 'The Literary Apprenticeship of Clemence of Barking', *AUMLA (Journal of the Australasian Universities Language and Literature Association)*, 9 (1958), 3–22.

39 J. Wogan-Browne, 'An Unnoticed Quotation from Clemence of Barking' (forthcoming).

40 For much of what follows we are indebted to *VCH Essex* (London: Constable, 1907), vol. II pp. 115–22.

41 On the architectural resources of nunneries in general, see Roberta Gilchrist, *Gender and Material Culture: The Archaeology of Religious Women* (London and New York: Routledge, 1994).

42 Young, *Drama of the Medieval Church*, vol. I, pp. 166–7.

43 Eamon Duffy, *The Stripping of the Altars: Traditional Religion in England, c.1400–1580* (New Haven and London: Yale University Press, 1992), pp. 430–1).

44 *Aldhelm: The Prose Works*, trans. M. Lapidge and M. Herren (Cambridge: Brewer, 1979), p. 59.

45 See *Bede: A History of the English Church and People*, trans. Sherley-Price, bk IV, chs 6–10, pp. 217–23.

46 Marvin L. Colker, 'Lives by Jocelin of Canterbury associated with Barking Abbey', *Studia Monastica*, 7 (1965), 383–460 (p. 388).

47 *The Letters of Osbert of Clare, Prior of Westminster*, ed. E. W. Williamson (London: Oxford University Press, 1929), letters 42, 21, 22.

48 See M. Dominica Legge, *Anglo-Norman Literature and its Background* (Oxford: Oxford University Press, 1963; repr. Westport, Conn.: Greenwood Press, 1978), p. 188.

49 *La Vie de saint Thomas Becket*, ed. E. Walberg (Lund: Glemp, 1922), p. 8, stanza 33.

50 A. I. Doyle, 'Books connected with the Vere Family and Barking Abbey', *Transactions of the Essex Archaeological Society*, 25 (1958), 222–43.

lv

51 Some sources and analogues have been suggested in Batt. See also notes to vv. 785–804, 965–1000.

52 *Marie de France: Fables*, ed. and trans. Harriet Spiegel (Toronto: University of Toronto Press, 1987); *Les Proverbes de Salemon*, ed. C. Isoz, 3 vols, ANTS 44, 45, 50 (London: ANTS, 1988–94), vol. III, pp. 11–18.

53 Her better-known contemporary Chrétien de Troyes opens his *Erec et Enide* in a similar way. See *Chrétien de Troyes: Erec et Enide*, ed. and trans. C. W. Carroll (New York and London: Garland, 1987), pp. 2–3, vv. 4–8; and Glyn S. Burgess, *Chrétien de Troyes: Erec et Enide* (London: Grant and Cutler, 1984), 'The Prologue', pp. 9–14.

54 For an edition of the text in MS Rylands French 6, see Fawtier-Jones, 'Les Vies de Sainte Catherine,' pp. 101–3. On possible parallels between the two texts, see MacBain, pp. xiii–iv; and note to v. 35 of the present translation. Bray, 'The Legend of Saint Katherine', pp. 64–6, questions MacBain's identification of the text in MS Rylands French 6 as Clemence's vernacular source.

55 Simon Gaunt, *Gender and Genre in Medieval French Literature* (Cambridge: Cambridge University Press, 1995), pp. 228–33 (p. 231).

56 See R. W. Southern, *St Anselm and his Biographer: A Study of Monastic Life and Thought, 1059–c.1130* (Cambridge: Cambridge University Press, 1963), ch. 2 (pp. 34–8), ch.3 (pp. 93–102).

57 See MacBain, 'Five Old French Renderings of the *Passio sancte Katerine*', pp. 57–63; Batt; and Legge, *Anglo-Norman Literature and its Background*, pp. 67–8.

58 See W. MacBain, 'Some Religious and Secular Uses of the Vocabulary of *fin'amor* in the Early Decades of the Northern French Narrative Poem', *French Forum*, 13 (1988), 261–76, pp. 270–4, and 'Courtliness in some Religious Texts of the Twelfth Century', in *L'Imaginaire courtois et son double*, ed. Giovanna Angeli and Luciano Formisano (Salerno: Edizioni Scientifiche italiane, 1992), pp. 371–86.

59 See Caroline Walker Bynum, *Jesus as Mother: Studies in the Spirituality of the High Middle Ages* (Berkeley, Los Angeles and London: University of California Press, 1982), esp. ch. 4. For an analysis of the hero as mother in modern romance, see Radway, *Reading the Romance*, ch. 4 ('The ideal romance'), esp. pp. 135–40.

60 Bernard, *De diligendo Deo*, in *S. Bernardi: Opera omnia*, III, ed. J. Leclercq and H. M. Rochais (Rome: Editiones Cistercienses, 1963), esp. pp. 132–3; Augustine, *Confessions*, I, chs 2, 5; Anselm, *De beatitudine* in *Memorials of St Anselm*, ed. R. W. Southern and F. S. Schmitt, Auctores britannici medii aevi, 1 (London: Oxford University Press for the British Academy, 1969), pp. 285/30–286/11.

61 Batt, pp. 105, 108.

62 This is not to suggest that a radicalized notion of class is entertained in

Catherine. It remains a feudal and courtly text, and references to the common good are conventionally Christian.

63 See Aviad M. Kleinberg, *Prophets in their Own Country: Living Saints and the Making of Sainthood in the Later Middle Ages* (Chicago and London: University of Chicago Press, 1992). For the doctrinal and cultural importance of the body and its integrity, see Caroline Walker Bynum, *The Resurrection of the Body in Western Christianity, 200–1336* (New York: Columbia University Press, 1995), parts II and III, and 'Material Continuity, Personal Survival, and the Resurrection of the Body: A Scholastic Discussion in its Medieval and Modern Contexts', in her *Fragmentation and Redemption: Essays on Gender and the Human Body in Medieval Religion* (New York: Zone Books, 1992), pp. 239–97.

64 MacBain, 'Five Old French Renderings of the *Passio sancte Katerine*', p. 57.

65 See, for example, Brenda M. Bolton, '*Vitae matrum*: A Further Aspect of the *Frauenfrage*', in *Medieval Women*, ed. D. Baker (Oxford: Blackwell, 1978), pp. 253–73; and J. Coakley, 'Friars as Confidants of Holy Women in Medieval Dominican Hagiography', in *Images of Sainthood in Medieval Europe*, ed. R. Blumenfeld-Kosinski and T. Szell (Ithaca and London: Cornell University Press, 1991), pp. 222–46.

66 Caroline Walker Bynum, '"And woman his humanity": Female Imagery in the Religious Writing of the Later Middle Ages'; orig. publ. in *Gender and Religion: On the Complexity of Symbols*, ed. C. W. Bynum, S. Harrell and P. Richman (Boston, Mass.: Beacon Press, 1986); repr. in Bynum, *Fragmentation and Redemption*, pp. 151–79.

67 The number of deacons was raised to fourteen in the eleventh century. See note to v. 128.

68 H. Delehaye, 'Recherches sur le légendier romain: *La Passion de S. Polychronius*', *Analecta Bollandiana*, 51 (1933), 70–1.

69 The discrepant papal and secular reigns are carefully considered, though not resolved, by Jacobus de Voragine in his influential thirteenth-century *Legenda aurea* (see note to v. 95).

70 This is the Antiphon for Benedictus at Lauds on St Lawrence's day (identified in *Letters of Osbert of Clare*, ed. Williamson, p. 214, no. 22, p. 95 n. 3; cf. Psalms 16:3.

71 *De officiis ministrorum, PL,* 16.91–2; trans. H. de Romestin *et al.* as 'Duties of the Clergy', in *Select Library of Nicene and Post-Nicene Fathers of the Church*, 2nd ser. (1896; repr. Grand Rapids, Mich.: Eerdmans, 1955), I, ch. 41, p. 35.

72 *The Letters of D. H. Lawrence*, I, ed. James T. Boulton (Cambridge: Cambridge University Press, 1979), p. 519.

73 The following information is taken chiefly from Réau, *L'Iconographie*, t. III, pt 2, pp. 787–92.

74 *Bede: A History of the English Church and People*, trans. Sherley-Price, bk III, ch. 29.

75 See *Ælfric's Lives of Saints*, ed. W. W. Skeat, EETS, OS 94 and 114 (London: Kegan Paul, Trench, Trübner for EETS, 1890–1900; repr. in 1 vol. 1966), p. 332, v. 241.

76 William of Malmesbury, *Gesta pontificum*, p. 6; and Ziolkowski.

77 Later prose French lives of Lawrence occur in thirteenth- and fourteenth-century continental legendaries (see Paul Meyer, 'Légendes en prose', in *Histoire littéraire de France* (Paris: Imprimerie Nationale, 1906), XXXIII, pp. 378–458). For a list of verse and prose lives in English, see d'Evelyn, 'Legends of Individual Saints', p. 603.

78 Stephen K. Wright, 'Is the Ashmole Fragment a Remnant of a Saint's Play?', *Neophilologus*, 75 (1991), 139–49 (pp. 142–3).

79 For Gerald of Wales, see *The Jewel of the Church: A Translation of Gemma Ecclesiastica by Giraldus Cambrensis*, trans. J. J. Hagen (Leiden: Brill, 1979), bk. II, ch. 33, p. 247. On Langland's use of Lawrence (in *Piers Plowman* C II. 127–36; XXVII. 64–71), see M. Teresa Tavormina, '*Piers Plowman* and the Liturgy of St Lawrence: Composition and Revision in Langland's Poetry', *Studies in Philology*, 84 (1987), 245–71.

80 *De gestis regum anglorum*, ed. William Stubbs, RS 90 (London: Eyre and Spottiswoode for HM Stationery Office, 1887), vol. I, ch. ii, p. 234; trans. J. A. Giles, *William of Malmesbury's Chronicle of the Kings of England* (London: Bell and Daldy, 1866), p. 212.

81 See *Letters of Osbert of Clare*, ed. Williamson, letter 22, pp. 93–6.

82 *The Ordinale and Customary of the Benedictine Nunnery of Barking Abbey*, ed. J. B. L. Tolhurst, vol. II, HBS 66 (London: HBS, 1928), p. 386, n. to p. 274.

83 Donovan, *The de Brailes Hours*, pp. 61–2.

84 Ibid., pp. 120–4, and figs 82–5.

85 Legge, *Anglo-Norman Literature and its Background*, p. 251.

86 This copy was not itself the original twelfth-century text, but a copy at one or more removes. On the manuscripts and textual tradition of the life, see Russell, pp. 1–6, and on the Egerton manuscript see also Russell, 'The Manuscript Source of the Fragment, Rylands French MS 6'.

87 Ed. H. Delehaye, in 'Recherches sur le légendier romain', *Analecta Bollandiana*, 51 (1933), 43–98, pp. 80–93.

88 See Meyer, 'Légendes en prose'.

89 On these versions, see Russell, p. 25 n. 44.

90 The relevant section of Philippe de Thaon's poem is printed in Russell, p. 62 n. 1. For a more recent edition, see *Comput (MS BL Cotton Nero A.V)*, ed. Ian Short, ANTS Plain Texts Series 2 (London: ANTS, 1984).

91 Details are given in the Notes to the Text (see esp. n. 15).

92 On the Latinity of some twelfth- and thirteenth-century holy women in Britain and the production of vernacular texts for them, see Bella Millett, 'Women in No Man's Land: English Recluses and the Development of Vernacular Literature in the Twelfth and Thirteenth Centuries', in *Women and Literature in Britain 1150–1500*, ed. Meale, pp. 86–103.

93 Eusebius, *Ecclesiastical History*, v, 52 (Bibbas); v, 26 (Attalus), trans. Deferrari, I (1953), pp. 278–9, 285. Examples are collected in Delehaye, 'Recherches sur le légendier romain', pp. 57–8.

94 Miri Rubin, *Corpus Christi: The Eucharist in Late Medieval Culture* (Cambridge: Cambridge University Press, 1991), pp. 122–6, 359–60; Cecil Roth, *A History of the Jews in England*, 3rd edn (Oxford: Clarendon Press, 1964), pp. 9, 56–7.

95 *Jewel of the Church*, trans. Hagen, bk 1, ch. 54, p. 125.

96 These connections are further underlined by an addition of the Anglo-Norman writer. At the end of the mourning for Lawrence, and in an addition to the *Passion of Polychronius*, the Anglo-Norman text has the priest Justinus say Mass and give communion (*Corpus Christi*, 'the body of Christ', v. 939) in the saint's memory.

97 See note to *Lawrence*, v. 128.

98 *The Early South English Legendary: MS Laud 108 in the Bodleian Library*, ed. C. Horstmann, EETS, os 87 (London: Trübner for the EETS, 1887), p. 343, v. 109.

99 M. Mollat, *The Poor in the Middle Ages: An Essay in Social History*, trans. A. Goldhammer (New Haven and London: Yale University Press, 1986), p. 111. Joel Rosenthal, *The Purchase of Paradise: Gift-giving and the Aristocracy, 1307–1485* (London: Routledge, 1972) deals with a later period, but is generally illuminating on medieval attitudes.

100 See *La Vie d'Edouard le confesseur*, ed. Södergaard, esp. vv. 851–1080, 2285–2456, 3075–3256, 3629–92.

101 Religious lyrics solicit contemplation of Christ by both men and women, but many are specifically addressed to women, and those which represent the Virgin as speaker focus a specifically female gaze on Christ's body (see Sarah Stanbury, 'The Virgin's Gaze: Spectacle and Transgression in Middle English Lyrics of the Passion', *PMLA*, 106 (1991), 1083–93). Prescriptive treatises enjoin special meditation on Christ's body for women. See, for example, Aelred of Rievaulx's treatise for his sister (ed. and trans. C. Dumont, *La Vie de recluse: La prière pastorale* (Paris: Editions du Cerf, 1961), pp. 104, 138–44) and *Guide*

for Anchoresses (see n. 4 above), part VII. Crucifixes displaying Christ's body were common in holy women's cells and in psalter illustrations, as well as in more public church iconography. For a study of this theme in a later period, see Sarah Beckwith, *Christ's Body: Identity, Culture and Society in Late Medieval Writings* (London and New York: Routledge, 1993).

102 *Vulgate*, pp. 176/627–177/628 (hereafter referred to by page and line number in the text).

103 See MacBain, p. 1, vv. 19–20, and *app. crit.*

104 For recent discussion see Bernadette A. Masters, 'Anglo-Norman in Context: The Case for Scribes', *Exemplaria*, 6 (1994), 167–203; *The Anglo-Norman Lyric: An Anthology*, ed. and trans. David L. Jeffrey and Brian J. Levy (Toronto: Pontifical Institute of Mediaeval Studies, 1990), pp. 17–27.

105 Ian Robinson, *Chaucer's Prosody* (Cambridge: Cambridge University Press, 1976), ch. 8, esp. pp. 151–6.

106 See Russell, *La Vie de saint Laurent*, pp. 19–21.

SUGGESTIONS FOR FURTHER READING

General: Historical and Literary Context

M. Dominica Legge, *Anglo-Norman Literature and its Background* (Oxford: Clarendon Press, 1963; repr. Westport, Conn.: Greenwood Press, 1978) is the basic modern survey of Anglo-Norman Literature. Her *Anglo-Norman in the Cloisters* (Edinburgh: Edinburgh University Press, 1950) is also still useful. These works should be supplemented by the important article by Ian Short, 'Patrons and Polyglots: French Literature in Twelfth-Century England', *Anglo-Norman Studies*, 14 (1992), 229–49.

A good introduction to British culture of the post-Conquest period is Elizabeth Salter, *English and International: Studies in the Literature, Art and Patronage of Medieval England*, ed. Derek Pearsall and Nicolette Zeeman (Cambridge: Cambridge University Press, 1988), part I, chs 1 and 2.

Women and Literature in Britain, 1150–1500, ed. Carol M. Meale (Cambridge: Cambridge University Press, 1993) is a fundamental collection in which the essay by Jocelyn Wogan-Browne, '"Clerc u lai, muïne u dame": Women and Anglo-Norman Hagiography in the Twelfth and Thirteenth Centuries' (pp. 61–85), provides background pertinent to the present volume.

For the history of women religious, see Sally Thompson, *Women Religious: The Founding of English Nunneries after the Norman Conquest* (Oxford: Clarendon Press, 1992), ch. 9; Sharon K. Elkins, *Holy Women of Twelfth-Century England* (Chapel Hill, NC.: University of North Carolina Press, 1988).

Saints and Saints' Lives

An invaluable reference work is D. H. Farmer, *The Oxford Dictionary of Saints* (Oxford: Clarendon Press, 1978, etc.). There has been no comprehensive modern literary history of hagiography in England since Theodor Wolpers, *Die englische Heiligenlegenden des Mittelatlers* (Tübingen: Niemeyer, 1964), but extant lives are listed in Charlotte d'Evelyn, 'Legends of Individual Saints', in *Manual of the Writings in Middle English*, ed. J. Burke Severs (Hamden, Conn.: Archon Books, 1967–) fasc. 2 (1970), pp. 514ff. Recent collections of articles giving some indication of the range and variety of the genre include *The South English Legendary: A Critical Assessment*, ed. Klaus P. Jankofsky (Tübingen: Francke, 1992); *Images of Sainthood in Medieval Europe*, ed. Renate Blumenfeld-Kosinski and Timea Szell (Ithaca and London: Cornell University Press, 1991). André Vauchez, *La Sainteté en occident aux derniers siècles du moyen âge* (Rome: Ecole française de Rome, 1980) is a fundamental study of medieval sanctity. For Anglo-Norman saints' lives in a European context, see Martine Thirry-Stassin, 'L'Hagiographie anglo-normande', in her *Hagiographies: Histoire internationale de la littérature hagiographique latine et vernaculaire en Occident des origines à 1500*, ed. G. Philippart (Turnhout: Brepols, forthcoming). A fundamental modern work on European saints' lives and women's use of them is Caroline Walker Bynum, *Holy Feast and Holy Fast: The Religious Significance of Food to Medieval Women* (Berkeley, Los Angeles and London: University of California Press, 1987).

Clemence of Barking

Catherine Batt, 'Clemence of Barking's Transformations of *courtoisie* in *La Vie de sainte Catherine d'Alexandrie*', in *Translation in the Middle Ages*, ed. Roger Ellis (*New Comparisons*, 12 (1991), 102–33).

William MacBain, 'Anglo-Norman Women Hagiographers', in *Anglo-Norman Anniversary Essays*, ed. Ian Short, ANTS Occasional Publications 2 (London: ANTS, 1993), pp. 235–50.

———'The Literary Apprenticeship of Clemence of Barking', *AUMLA* (*Journal of the Australasian Universities Language and Literature Association*), 9 (1958), 3–22.

Duncan Robertson, 'Writing in the Textual Community: Clemence of Barking's Life of St. Catherine', *French Forum* 21 (1966), 5–28.

Editions and Translations

Brigitte Cazelles, *The Lady as Saint: A Collection of French Hagiographic Romances of the Thirteenth Century* (Philadelphia, Pa: University of Pennsylvania Press, 1991). Includes Anglo-Norman and continental texts.

St Catherine

The Life of St. Catherine by Clemence of Barking, ed. William MacBain ANTS 18 (Oxford: Blackwell for the ANTS, 1964). A new edition and facing translation by Professor MacBain is planned for the ANTS's Occasional Publications series.

For other French lives of Catherine, see William MacBain, 'Five Old French Renderings of the *Passio sancte Katerine virginis*', in *Medieval Translators and their Craft*, ed. Jeanette Beer, Studies in Medieval Culture 25 (Kalamazoo, Mich.: University of Western Michigan, Medieval Institute Publications, 1989), pp. 41–63.

For the early Middle English Catherine life and an edition of the Vulgate Latin life, see *Seinte Katerine*, ed. S. R. T. O. d'Ardenne and E. J. Dobson, EETS, ss 7 (Oxford: EETS, 1981). For a translation of this early Middle English life, see *Anchoritic Spirituality: Ancrene Wisse and Associated Texts*, trans. Anne Savage and Nicholas Watson (New York and Mahwah, NJ: Paulist Press, 1991).

St Lawrence

La Vie de saint Laurent: An Anglo-Norman Poem of the Twelfth Century, ed. D. W. Russell, ANTS 34 (London: ANTS, 1976).

De saint Laurent: Poème anglo-normand du XIIe siècle, ed. Werner Söderhjelm (Paris: Welter, 1888) includes an account of the literary history of the legend.

Passio SS. Xystii et Laurentii, ed. H. Delehaye, in his 'Recherches sur le légendier romain', *Analecta Bollandiana*, 51 (1933), 43–98, pp. 80–93.

Anglo-Norman Lives by Women

La Vie d'Edouard le confesseur: Poème anglo-normand du XIIe siècle, ed. O. Södergaard (Uppsala: Almqvist & Wiksell, 1948).

   La Vie sainte Audrée: Poème anglo-normand du XIIIe siècle, ed. O. Södergaard (Uppsala: Almqvist & Wiksell, 1955).

NOTE ON THE TEXTS

Experiments with translation into English octosyllabics left us unconvinced that we could fairly represent these poems by such means. We have translated into modern English prose, seeking always as clearly and closely as possible to represent the meaning of the original and such of its stylistic effects as survive the loss of the original poetic form. We have not followed changes of narrative tense. For the *Life of St. Catherine* we have used the edition by William MacBain, *The Life of St. Catherine by Clemence of Barking*, ANTS 18 (Oxford, 1964), which takes Paris, Bibliothèque Nationale, MS nouv. acq. fr. 4503, as its base-text. Occasionally we have preferred readings from London, British Library, MS Additional 70513 (formerly Welbeck IC1). These are marked with an asterisk and discussed in the Notes to the Translation. For the *Life of St Lawrence* we have used the critical edition of Paris, Bibliothèque Nationale, MS f. fr. 19525, edited by D. W. Russell, *La Vie de saint Laurent: An Anglo-Norman Poem of the Twelfth Century*, ANTS 34 (London: ANTS, 1976). Latin words and phrases included in this text have been printed in italics in the text of the translation. For both texts, we have taken account of medieval punctuation and paragraphing as presented in the extant manuscripts, but have made further paragraph divisions as necessary for ease of reading in the translations.

VIRGIN LIVES
AND HOLY DEATHS

All those who know and understand what is good have a duty to demonstrate it wisely, so that by the fruit of its goodness others may be encouraged to do good deeds and to want what is good, as far as they are able.[1] For he who alone is good by his very nature gave us both precept and example. He wished not to conceal his goodness from us, but to reveal it publicly. His goodness suffices for everyone, for it alone is common to all. From his great bounty he feeds us, and all our goodness has its source in his goodness.[2] Blessed is he who turns to him and bends his heart to this great goodness which does not change with changing times or suffer reproach or attack from human law. Never did he fail anyone who desired him. A very rich prize is to be won in him who is and was and ever shall be. Now let us beseech him that in his grace he will allow us to perform this task and so follow his example here below that we shall see him face to face, where he reigns in majesty, one God in Holy Trinity. (1–28)

Because he is merciful it is right that he should assist me with this work, in which I intend to tell of someone who truly loved him and to translate her life, transposing it from Latin into the vernacular, so that it will be more pleasing to those who hear it. It was translated before and well set out according to the standards of the time.[3] But people then were not so hard to please or so critical as they are in our day, and will be even more so after we are gone. Because times and men's quality have changed, the poem is held in low esteem, for it is somewhat defective in places.[4] So it is necessary to correct it and to make the times conform to the people. I am not correcting it out of arrogance, for I seek no acclaim. He alone should be praised from whom I derive my small amount of knowledge. (29–50)

As we are told by the histories which set forth the events of the past, in Rome there was once an emperor of immense power. His father's name was Constantius, and his mother was the good Helen.[5] He himself bore the name Constantine, and the entire realm was under his sway. He granted peace to the holy church after reigning for ten years. It was he who defeated Maxentius, who had wrongfully seized power, making him flee as far as Alexandria, where he reigned for thirty-five years.[6] After these thirty-five years he was the cause of much suffering for the Christians. One day, as he was sitting in his palace, he fell into an evil train of thought and wanted to translate his thoughts into acts, for a wicked man cannot conceal his nature; when he sees an opportunity for evil deeds he is quite incapable of restraining himself.[7] And this is what Maxentius did, since he possessed the power to do so and was unable to conceal his iniquity. He then revealed his plans to his advisers, for it was through these men that he would put them into action. His messengers carried the announcement to everyone within his domain. (51–78)

Their proclamation began thus: 'The great Emperor Maxentius sends greetings to one and all. Whether he is loved or feared, let everyone come to court to hear his will and carry it out. If anyone speaks out against him, he will have no escape from death.' These words were heard and the threat was greatly feared. Whether from love or fear, everyone assembled on the appointed day. They all gathered at the pretorium,[8] as they had been commanded to do. (79–92)

The next day the king arrived with his counsellors and his favourites. He took his seat before his palace,[9] and his provost read out his proclamation: 'My lords, come to the temple where you will make sacrifices to the gods, when the priests cense the altars in the temple, and the king makes his handsome offering; beware lest anyone delay making his sacrifice to the gods, each according to his means.' He finished speaking, and many liked and welcomed what he said. Those who were wicked and sycophantic thought it was right. For it is natural for a wicked man, when he hears evil, to praise it, since his blame is redoubled when he reproaches in others what he feels within himself. It is fitting that the wicked should praise evil, and the good fear it. Because fear of death urged them on, they accompanied the pagans to the temple.[10] The emperor entered with a number of his counsellors. There he sacrificed a hundred and thirty bulls to the gods and invoked their aid. The kings, the counts and the barons doubled their gifts in order to please him. They offered bulls and sheep to the gods, and others did likewise. The poor brought birds and sacrificed them to the gods. The bellowing and the cries of the animals, living or dying, were so loud that the whole city resounded and all around the earth trembled. (93–132)

In the city of Alexandria, where they were carrying out this iniquity, there lived a young girl of high rank and great beauty.[11] The maiden was eighteen years old, and her name was Catherine. Her father was a king during his lifetime and he had no other son or daughter. He had her taught letters and how to argue a case and defend her position. There was no dialectician on earth who could defeat her in argument.[12] She was very wise in the ways of this world, but her heart was set on higher things. In God she placed her whole mind, her worth and her fair youth, and she showed disdain for all mortal lovers, devoting herself to an immortal lover whose love is chaste and pure and everlasting in its delight. In this delight there is no pain, for its joy is never illusory. This blessed maiden, who was wholly given over to God, set her mind on this joy, which is not subject to the whims of fortune.[13] Her father, when he died, left her his entire kingdom, and she maintained it wisely and kept his household around her. She shared out all his wealth, for God alone was sufficient for her.[14] She gave no thought to any other treasure, but fixed her heart entirely on him. She was of noble heart and lineage, and in God she was made perfect and wise. (133–68)

One day, she sat in the city mentioned above and heard a loud clamour. Somewhat frightened by this, she asked her attendants what it might be. They told her the truth about it, and when she heard this news you may be sure that it was not at all pleasing to her. She went straight out of her palace and with her attendants came to the temple, where she saw Christians weeping, groaning and lamenting. They were there because they feared for their lives and they were making sacrifices along with the others. The heart of anyone who heard the noise and

the grief burnt with great anguish. She bowed her fair head a
little and silently worshipped God. She felt great sorrow in her
heart, but wisely restrained herself. This beloved of God thought
that she would take the king to task and prove to him by logic
that he and his law were worthy of condemnation.[15] Confident
in God and in her own intelligence, she entered the temple
without fear. Seeing the tyrant seated high above everyone else,
she raised her hand, crossed herself and went straight towards
him. She was well trained in fair speech and began her address
as follows: 'Emperor, your rank demands that you receive a
greeting. If you were willing to honour God, who can damn or
save you, and to love him alone, and to serve with all your heart
the one who brought about your birth and will bring about your
death, and if you had within you the faculty of reason, you
would not worship anything other than him alone. But, instead,
you worship the images made of him by his creatures. What you
worship was made by man: they were given limbs and a body,
but not intelligence. They can neither see nor hear; they have no
power for good or evil; they do no good to their friends and no
harm to their enemies.[16] And yet you worship them humbly.
Tell me the reason, for I cannot understand it.' (169–218)

The maiden broke off her speech and the emperor rose
slightly. He turned towards her and became thoughtful, fixing
his eyes on her beautiful face. She seemed to him to be beautiful,
fair-complexioned and well instructed in the art of speaking.
After a little while, he gave her his answer appropriately, in
accordance with his religion. 'Fair one,' he said, 'you speak very
well, but there is little sense in what you say. You cannot prove
your claims, nor condemn our faith in this way. We have taken
this faith which we uphold from our ancestors, who were
masters and princes of Rome; they were the embodiment of
religious authority. But your faith is so cruel and so deadly for
all its believers. There is no greater horror or more dreadful
error than when you say that Jesus Christ took our mortal flesh
on earth, that he had to be put on the cross to save the living
and the dead, and that on the third day he had to rise from the
dead and speak to his disciples. You and your people say this,
but we do not accept it, nor do our people. This error is not
sufficient for you, since you despise our gods, who are and will

remain immortal and who will continue for ever and ever. What people is so lacking in faith and what land so remote that it does not sacrifice to the sun, humbly invoking its favour and sacrificing to the moon in similar fashion? These are the gods in whom I believe. Now it is up to you to respond.' (219–58)

The maiden listened to him and gave a faint smile. Very gently and courteously she said to him: 'Your error is very great because it does not address the truth. How could you believe in the son, when you despise God his father, whose power is experienced by the whole of creation, the land and the sea and everything pertaining to them? The heavens, the sun, the moon and each and every star give praise to the creator, each according to its capacity. The sun shines when he makes it shine, for he existed before it did. He makes the moon hold its course and wax and wane at his pleasure. Everything renders service to him in accordance with the dictates of reason, and you would have great cause to fear for yourself if you could reflect on how you have scorned the creator, who has lent you such great honour. He has made your power so extensive that you have been exalted in this kingdom. King, you can draw on this as an example: if any of your people, to whom you had done great honour and in whom you had invested lordship over important affairs, wished to offend you, and in their great power did not acknowledge you as their lord but went on to serve someone else of much lower rank, you would avenge yourself very cruelly, when the opportunity arose.[17] So he who alone is God and alone is king should take vengeance on you, since you have deserted him for his image and worship his creation. What you worship is worthless, for you will never derive any benefit from it. So abandon this error, in which you can find no truth. No one should choose error if he cannot put it to good advantage. You ought to abandon this error, since you cannot establish the truth of it.' (259–304)

Having listened to her, the tyrant marvelled and prepared to make an appropriate response: 'Fair one,' he said, 'it is apparent to me that you possess great knowledge. But you would be very much wiser if, from your earliest years, you had acquired your philosophy, which is so firmly implanted in you, from our masters. I do not think that your equal in expounding and

proving an argument would have existed on earth. I am con-
vinced that you would be favourable towards our gods if you
knew the truth about them. But you must wait a little, for we
have not yet completed the sacred rites owed to our gods, to
whom I am performing this sacrifice.'[18] Having said this, he
departed and summoned his personal clerks. He told them his
wishes in this matter and they set it down in writing. At the
beginning he had greetings placed and then the text read as
follows:[19] 'Let it be known by everyone far and near – especially
rhetoricians, who are experts in fine and effective speech[20] – that
the emperor has a great need for everyone to come to him and
maintain his honour and his law, for he finds himself confronted
by a powerful woman advocating that he should abandon his
law.[21] If they can confound her so that she can make no further
reply and has to surrender publicly, when she prides herself so
much on her skills in debate, he will make them his personal
advisers and they will be honoured above all others.' (305–42)

When the letters were written and read out to the emperor,
they were duly sealed with the stone in his ring. Then they were
given to messengers, who took them to the clerks. When he had
completed his sacred rites, the emperor gave orders for her to be
seized and taken to the royal palace. She found favour with
everyone and was greatly praised; even the emperor felt great
tenderness towards her. He would gladly have elevated her to
his own rank, if she had been willing to worship his gods.[22] He
cajoled her with fine words, for in his heart he had a great desire
for her. First he gazed upon her, then addressed her: 'Tell me
what your name is, fair maiden,' he said, 'and where you were
born and of what family. I do not know you or your lineage,
but your countenance is very royal. This royal brow I see
proclaims you a king's daughter. I do not know from what
masters you have received instruction, but you are a great credit
to them. You are adorned with every art and illumined with
every quality, except for your refusal to love our powerful and
immortal gods.' (343–72)

To this the maiden, who was entirely given over to God, now
replied: 'Emperor, if you seek to know my name, I am called
Catherine. My father was truly a king and he had no son or
daughter but me. He had me instructed in all the arts, in such a

way that I have a command of them all. I had good masters who were powerful men, clever in debate and noble in heart. In all that pertained to worldly renown they were truly distinguished. But when I heard the substance of my beloved's gospel, I came to hold their learning in very low esteem, for I am completely devoted to him. I have given all my love to him, in return for his love which pleases me so much. Him alone I worship in the Trinity, three persons in unity, for he alone is God and saviour.[23] For this reason, lord emperor, you must provide a very convincing reason if I am to worship your gods, who have no consciousness of what they are; they do nothing to benefit themselves or others. They cannot hear, speak, see, feel or think. Oh, what noble gods are these! Emperor, I therefore beg you, since you can produce no good reason, to tell me why I should worship them.' (373–404)

With this the maiden fell silent. Just then the news arrived that the messengers had returned with the masters. There were fifty of them, all of subtle mind; at that time there were none better on earth. Presently they came into the palace and greeted the emperor, who welcomed them warmly, for he was greatly heartened by their arrival. He examined them intently and put them to the test; their intelligent approach to things pleased him. They wondered greatly why he had tested them in that way. With one voice they asked the reason why they had come, and he replied: 'I shall tell you the business on which I summoned you. I have here with me a maiden who scorns my gods and my law. She is very young, but she displays as much intelligence as if she had lived a long time. She knows the nature of every art, its meaning, its explanation and its methods of proof. She prides herself on debating, and no mortal can surpass her. She has vanquished many people in such a way that they were reduced to silence. But it distresses me a great deal more that she has so dishonoured my gods that she considers them to be man-made and the false cult of the devil. I could easily have her destroyed and silence her fine speech, but I should deem it a greater honour to have her vanquished in debate, and if she then refuses to obey us or serve our gods, I shall seek such torments for her that her arguments will be of little worth. My lords, I have summoned you for this purpose; I am grateful to you for coming. If you can vanquish her, you will receive very great honours. You will be

my counsellors in all things or have whatever else you would
like'. (405–50)

The tyrant ceased speaking, and one of the clerks rose. To
him the cause for which they had been summoned seemed
outrageous. He was very wicked and arrogant, and also jealous
of the good things he had heard about her. To this day many
people feel great chagrin at virtues possessed by others. When
the good receive more praise than they do, they feel that they
are being reproached. An arrogant man cannot admit that
someone is his equal in goodness unless it be someone who
enjoys his favour, shares his habits and follows his example. If
he knows what is good, he refuses to declare it; if another
proclaims it, he refuses to listen. When he hears others praised,
he often takes on something he later regrets. That is what this
man did, as a result of the great envy he felt for God's beloved.
The good which he had heard about her made him take
something upon himself as a result of which he was later forced
to repent and to confess the real truth.[24] He took it upon himself
to speak for everyone, saying arrogantly to the king: 'Emperor,
I am utterly astonished that you have taken such wretched
advice and promised us such a great reward for vanquishing a
woman skilled in debate. We have travelled far and it was well
worth it on her account! How gloriously our names will be
remembered after such a victory! If one wretched clerk had
defeated her, that would have been quite enough effort
expended, and yet on her account the finest clerks on earth are
gathered here! Philosophers and grammarians, especially rhetoricians and good dialecticians, have come here for a truly
important matter. She will certainly be able to oppose them, to
lay out her arguments and demolish theirs! Whoever she is,
summon her, and we shall make her concede and confess that
she has never seen or heard men as wise as those she has found
here.' (451–98)

Everyone agreed with him, but that night they rested. The
maiden was kept under guard, as the tyrant had commanded. A
messenger told her what had been said in the palace and that
fifty clerks were there against whom she would have to dispute
alone. The handmaiden of God felt no fear; her good intent was
her comfort. Everyone should surely take comfort in good

intent. Good intent is never without effect, providing one draws contentment and power from it. Yet good intent can remain hidden when it is necessary. It is often out of fear that it hides, and often to its dishonour. Concealment is sensible when one is afraid of encountering evil. Nevertheless, God's beloved did not hide on account of fear. She placed her confidence and hope in him from whom she derived her good intent.[25] Humbly she sought help from him, and strength from his heavenly hosts.[26] She began her prayer softly, saying: 'O true wisdom, O lofty and true strength, hear me, O good Jesus! Look on your feeble handmaid, who calls upon you in her great need. Fair Lord, in your honour have I undertaken this battle. You are my comfort and my life; from you alone do I seek help. Lord, may your name be praised, you who have given us such comfort by the words of solace which you spoke to your elected ones: "When you are to be judged and stand before kings, do not think about what to say, and have no fear of them. I shall give you eloquence, knowledge and wisdom in speech."[27] Most high God, who spoke thus and did this honour to your own, grant, Lord, that I may speak in such a way that I shall be able to show your righteousness and overcome these tyrants, who have come here to vilify you. Lord, strike them all dumb, or else make them praise and confess your name, and make them know your power by the force of truth.' With this she finished her prayer, and the good Lord received it and comforted her by sending to her an angel who descended in such brightness that the entire place was illumined. The maiden was very fearful, but he said to her with great gentleness: 'Beloved of God, have no fear, for God has heard your prayer. He makes it known to you through me that he is with you and will remain with you everywhere. In the debate against his enemies, which you have undertaken on his behalf, you will most certainly have good sense and reason and eloquence in speech. Through his truth you will surely conquer them and you will make them believe in him in such a way that they will suffer death for him and come to him through martyrdom. Through the power of their great faith many will abandon their pagan beliefs. After this great victory, you will receive a crown of glory. Here you will suffer a transitory death, but there you will have eternal life. You will dwell for ever in the choir of virgins, where you will behold your spouse for evermore.'[28] Having said this, he departed and she comforted herself in God. (499–584)

The night passed and the dawn broke. The sun sent its beautiful rays aloft.[29] The tyrant rose early and, after having himself attired in regal garments, left his chamber in the palace and summoned his debaters. Then he ordered the maiden to come and prove her statements. She was delighted to be summoned and made her way quickly to the palace. When she entered in full view of everyone, they gazed upon her and marvelled at the inexpressible beauty through which her great goodness was manifested. For often one's countenance shows whether one is wicked or honourable, and a foolish appearance often indicates the folly which inhabits one's heart. Then again it can conceal itself under a feigned appearance of doing good. But folly which is overt is preferable to wickedness which is well hidden. Whoever hides evil until that evil is manifested makes himself known both too soon and too late. An appearance of folly makes the fool feared, and an appearance of good makes the worthy man loved. And this is why I tell you that all those who saw the maiden did just this. Everyone loved her for her beautiful appearance, and everyone praised her speech greatly. For you seldom see a foolish woman who does not reveal her folly in her speech. But no one could criticize this maiden in the matter of fine and eloquent discourse. Her gentle features demonstrated clearly the wisdom in her heart. At that time there was no one on earth as beautiful as this handmaiden of God. For love of her, all those who lived near the city assembled, some drawn by her beauty, others by her great goodness.[30] (585–626)

The tyrant sat on his throne, his face fierce and arrogant. Beside him sat the clerks, who displayed great arrogance. Their frivolous appearance clearly revealed the great pride in their heart. Inordinately proud and outrageous in demeanour, they laughed uproariously and mocked the maiden. The tyrant was very angry that the contest was so slow in starting. The maiden was not afraid; she made the sign of the cross over herself. Then everyone in the palace was ordered to fall silent and pay attention. The lady began her speech, saying to the evil villain Maxentius: 'This is not an even contest, when you have set against me alone fifty clerks who are experienced debaters, without peers on earth. Besides that, you promise them honour if they are strong enough to vanquish me, but you have promised nothing to me, whom you have pitted against them all alone. I have neither fear nor love because of your promise, for I claim my reward from him for whose love I am placed in the field and for whom I have undertaken this battle. But there is one thing I do want to ask you, and you cannot rightly refuse me: if my God gives me victory over your worldly glory, you will agree to worship him and serve him and love him.' He replied angrily: 'Fair one, it is not fitting for you to propose a convenant to me, and under my law I do not grant it to you'. (627–66)

The maiden realized that her entreaty was in vain. Presently she turned to the clerks and addressed them politely: 'My lords,' she said, 'if there is any rhetorician or good dialectician here, let him come forward to debate with me, since, as I believe, you have come here on my account. He will soon be able to put my skill to the test.' A philosopher, who thought more highly of himself than of any of the others, rose up at once.[31] He said to her with great arrogance: 'It is your place to start, for it is on your account that we have come here and been put to so much trouble. You must first reveal your wisdom to us, then you can be fearful about ours.' Smiling, the lady said to him: 'I certainly had little esteem for your wisdom, and since coming to know my God I have thought even less of it. Once I had heard him spoken of, I abandoned all your false arts, in which I was once so knowledgeable that for my age I had no equal on earth. I was well aware that they were empty of faith and far removed from the true path.[32] This was the reason why I committed myself to the good Jesus, who is salvation for his believers. This Jesus, our saviour, is the son of the sovereign father, through whom the father created all things and ordained them in his wisdom. He made men and women to be rational beings and then placed them in paradise. The enemy deceived the woman through the apple which she ate. She gave some to her husband.* He ate it and thereby went astray.[33] As a result of this disobedience, great sorrow arose in the world, in as far as everyone would have gone to hell when they died, whether they were good or bad. But the good God, who had created them, was merciful enough to take pity on them and so sent into the world his son, who saved us all by his death. He alone is lord, he alone is God, immortal in his nature. The son of God suffered death in the flesh; by his death he saved us from death. For us he suffered death temporarily; eternal life arose out of it for us. When he came down to earth, he clothed himself in flesh and blood, which he took from a chaste maiden; she was his creation and his handmaiden. Without defilement he placed himself in her, and without pain he was born of her.[34] What I have said is the truth; it is proved by many things. This is the essence of my position: I believe him to be both God and man. This is my philosophy; I know of no other of which I might now speak.' (667–732)

She had not even finished her speech when one of the clerks let out a great cry. He called upon all the citizens and the emperor who was in command of them: 'Lords, how long are we to suffer this foolish girl in our midst? We are repaying our gods poorly for the benefits we derive from them if we fail to avenge them on this girl, who has so reviled their name. I expected to hear great wisdom from her, and that was the reason why we were summoned here. She tells us the tale of Jesus, who long ago was hanged on the cross. One of his disciples betrayed him by selling him to the evil Jews. They decided to crucify him and they nailed his hands and feet. He could not escape death, for he was constrained to suffer it. On the third day he returned to life and afterwards ascended to heaven. This is what Christians go around saying and they consider him to be omnipotent. This girl also holds their erroneous view and she claims that he is the creator. She began her speech with him, but will have to end with someone else. She has started something which will not take her far.' (733–62)

When he had said this, she made her response, in the hearing of everyone who had heard what he said. 'In God's name,' she said, 'as I understand it, I did have a good beginning in him who created all things and who is the beginning of everything which is good. I did begin well, through him who is responsible for your existence and mine. This is not something with which you should reproach me in any way, if you wish to understand what is right. The reason why you want to refute my statements is that you cannot prove your own. Since you consider what I say mere invention, provide me with a rational demonstration of why you wish to censure me in this way, when you do not know how to correct me. Let me now have clear proof of it, for I shall listen to it without fail.'[35] (763–80)

He replied to her in great anger, scarcely knowing what to say: 'By my faith,' he said, 'I prove it to you by the fact that I find no truth in what you say.[36] If he is as you tell us, both God and man and the son of God, how can the son of God die or an immortal suffer death? By right he cannot die if his nature is immortal. If he was a man, then he is mortal and in no way equal to an immortal. He could not have died if he was God, nor come back to life if he was mortal. How can a man conquer death? And if God died, that was absurd. A mortal cannot escape death, nor an immortal suffer death. You show yourself to be against nature, for you are straying from the path of reason. I can grant that he is either God or man, but both together I find unjustifiable. He must be one or the other, for both he cannot be.'[37] (781–804)

When this clerk had finished speaking, she said to him, like the wise woman she was: 'Your ingenious argument is damaged by your contradiction of the truth. Because you refuse to believe, you present us with a pair of contraries. If he is man, then he is not God. If he is God, then he is not mortal. You refuse to allow that it could be true that Jesus is both God and man. If you wish to know the truth, remove what is superfluous, the great arrogance of your false understanding, for you have no rightful defence. Become a disciple in order to learn, and I shall make you understand the truth. You will see nothing with either heart or eye, if you have no doubt of this.[38] Now behold his creatures, both their being and their natures, for through them you can know his ineffable power. His power is manifested in them all; he alone provides sustenance for all. Since he made everything from nothing, and maintains everything by himself, and has power over everything, and has made everything as it pleased him, could he, who can do everything as he wishes, not then become a man? And can he not make himself what he made you and me? Through his power, not through nature, the maker became a creature. He became a man visible to all, for in himself he was God invisible. If he had not been a man, he could not have died, and if he had not been God, he could not have come back to life. In short, the essence of it is that the man was in God, and God in the man. The son of God suffered death in the flesh, and the flesh came back to life in God. He had revived mortals who had died a creaturely death by the demands of natural law;[39] could he not then bring himself back to life? He cleansed lepers and madmen and cured the sick and the blind. If you do not believe that Jesus Christ performed these miracles on earth, at least believe that in Jesus' name many men have had this power. (805–56) Through him many people have brought the dead to life and healed the sick by virtue of his name. He who gives such power to his followers must surely be believed to be God. How very great God's power must be in itself, when man acquires so much of it through his faith. He who gives power to others can certainly manifest it in himself. With this I prove to you clearly that Jesus is truly God. For we are well aware that if he were not God, he could not do this; and we know that Jesus was a man. So he is God and man through his power. And if Jesus experienced death, upon my faith, death did not conquer him. Death did not kill Jesus Christ, but rather Jesus killed death within himself. If you have any doubt about this, I shall provide you with yet another proof. (857–76) If you refuse to believe me, at least believe the demons who bear witness to my words and say that Jesus is the son of God, when they are summoned in his name in such a way that they speak the truth about him. They loathe speaking the truth, but his might deprives them of all their power so that they cannot hide the truth, and he makes them manifest it against their will. Wretch, how dreadful is your error in not believing in the creator, in whom, perceiving and fearing his power, even demons believe. In God's name, given the great wisdom I can see in you, I am astonished that you deny our God and scorn him and his cross in this manner. I shall relate two examples concerning the holy cross of Jesus Christ, which were written down by Plato and which I have found in your books.[40] He said that God would show himself in a form other than any then known and he would have a clear sign; this is the cross which confounds you.[41] Again, the Sibyl says of the cross (I know you have texts of her sayings): "Blessed," she says, "is that God who hangs fixed high on a tree."[42] She prophesied his coming, saying much about his birth and about his cross and his death. If you do not believe this, then you are wrong. Here you have an admission and clear proof of the truth from your own people. Plato said that God would come into the world and would appear in the form of a man. The Sybil said: "Blessed was that God who was hanged on the tree."[43] She called him blessed because she well knew that he would conquer death. I have told you the sayings of your own people because you would not believe ours or our holy scripture, which shows us everything which is right. If you refuse to believe your own writings, you will have difficulty in believing ours.' (877–924)

With that God's beloved fell silent and her opponent attacked her again. 'Surely,' he said, 'if it is true that your God has such power, he would never have allowed himself to be put on the cross. This I can use to contradict you and your learning. Why did he who could protect everyone from death need to die? How could death have power over him who was able to raise the dead? This I refute with confidence. If he is God, he did not die at all. If he was a man and did experience death, then I deny his resurrection. And if you wish to defend yourself against me on this point, you will need to acquire wisdom from someone else.' (925–40)

He fell silent and she said to him: 'From you I have learned very little.[44] I did consider you wise, but no more, for you are too violently opposed to what is right. I have no need of your knowledge and thus I contradict your statement. You are misled in this matter by your own philosophy, for you have not properly understood. I shall say again what I said before, although I have already proved what I say. My point is that God our saviour is by nature equal to the father, and since he is the father's equal he is not himself mortal. He cannot suffer death in himself, nor feel sorrow or suffering. Since he could not die in the nature in which he was, he covered himself in flesh and blood, which he received from a virgin's womb. He did not change his nature, but honoured ours by his own. His could not be harmed, but ours was exalted by his.[45] When the father, who sent him and who made everything from nothing, had created man and woman and given them power over good and evil, that man sinned through the fruit of the tree which God forbade him.[46] By this fruit we were damned and given over to a cruel death. Because God did not wish to allow man to perish in this way, he received the frail flesh of man in order to redress what had happened with the apple. Through the fruit of the forbidden tree the whole world was condemned to death. Jesus was the acceptable fruit and fecund for the whole world. This good fruit was put on the cross and it restored to paradise man who had been thrown out because of the forbidden fruit. By this fruit, we who were destroyed by the other were saved. Do you not think it right that he who conquered by means of the tree was then by that same means conquered himself, by the fruit which was hung on it once more? If the Enemy deceived man so that he tore the fruit from the tree, man then deceived the enemy through the fruit which he hung again on the tree; and if God had not helped man, man would never have saved the world. But since God made man, it was right that he should support man and avenge man through man, and the apple through the fruit. God could easily have preserved the world from the enemy through his power or through his will alone, but by a greater justice he did it this way, so that man avenged man. For a crime committed by man, man made amends. You should know that this reparation gives us hope of life, of living again after death. If you do not believe me now, you are wrong.'[47] (941–1010)

With this she fell silent. Everyone, great and small, marvelled at the way she had spoken and proved her claims rightfully. You should have heard all the people arguing, some denying what she said, other agreeing! If one said that she was right, another said rather that she was deceiving them. For it is customary with people that what one praises another attacks. If one speaks evil, another speaks good, for they are not all held by the same tether and they do not all spring from the same source. Nor is there anyone who finds favour with everyone; and if anyone does find it, it does not last, for such favour changes with circumstances. Often enough one sees people who are loved as long as they have great prosperity, but who have lost this favour entirely once their fortune has taken a turn for the worse. This love, which fails its friend at a time of need, is virtually worthless.[48]

Someone who, if rich, would be loved without deserving it, is hated because he is poor. A rich man is readily loved for next to nothing and greatly praised for a trifle, while if a poor person did the same thing, he would not win any praise or love by it. People are quicker to believe a rich man's error than a worthy man's truth. This was the case long ago and it still is, I believe, for people more readily lie out of fear than tell the truth out of love. They are more easily drawn to evil than to good. Many of the pagans behaved like this, for they held rather to what was false than to what was true. They feared the evil tyrant more than our good, all-powerful God. Many held back out of fear and thus withheld the truth. But all the clerks were abashed by the wisdom they saw in her. Her argument had given them so much understanding that they could no longer defend themselves.[49] (1011–56)

The king looked at the maiden and then addressed the clerks: 'Lords, what has happened to you?[50]* Have you all lost your wits? Why are you struck dumb and dismayed on account of a woman? Nothing like this has ever happened before. I think our gods do not care about us when you are all incapable of defending yourselves against a weak young girl. You are fifty men of great intellect, and against her you have no defence. There was never so great a shame as yours, if you are beaten. Lords,' he said, 'now reply. Defend my honour and my law, for we shall all end up being shamed if we do not win the victory.' (1057–74)

At this one of the clerks, who was very worthy and wise, replied: 'Truly,' he said, 'lord emperor, since our mothers bore us, we have never heard a woman speak so, or debate so wisely. She is not revealing foolish things to us, but matters full of truth. Her argument was mainly about the godhead.[51] No one with whom we might have debated was ever able to stand up to us so. He who thought himself wise at the outset thought himself a fool at the end. I have never seen a clerk, however skilled, whom I could not have forced to surrender. But I cannot refute her claims, for I see nothing wrong with them. It is no small thing that this lady advances against us. She speaks of the creator of the world and confounds our gods with the truth. We no longer know what to say to her, for our cause is false. We truly believe in her God, who created everything from nothing. From the moment this lady spoke to us about Jesus Christ's holy cross, his name, his power, his death and his birth, all our wisdom fled and we were completely overcome. We believe in him with all our hearts; we shall say nothing else to you.' (1075–1108)

The tyrant heard what he said and became very angry. He sighed deeply from the bottom of his heart and was filled with vexation. His heart became aflame with fierce rage. Then he commanded a great pyre to be constructed in the sight of all the inhabitants of the city and ordered the clerks to be bound and thrown into the fire all together. The pyre was quickly prepared and the clerks were seized and tightly bound. They were all soon led towards the blaze, but they did not fear a thing. One began to call out and cried to his fellows: 'Oh, dear companions, what shall we do, now that we believe in the good God who has done us such great honour that we have abandoned our error, who shows us the right way to live and who invites us to come to him by way of martyrdom? Let us first have ourselves baptized and blessed with his holy cross before we lose this life, which we lead with great sorrow.' Everyone cried out with one voice and called upon God's beloved to regenerate and cleanse them through baptism. (1109–36)

The maiden comforted them in kindly fashion and exhorted them to good deeds. 'Lords,' she said, 'do not be afraid. Take comfort in the creator and, I beg you, have no anxiety about baptism, my dear friends. You are all washed in the blood of God and reborn through his death. Through the flame which you see here you will receive the Holy Spirit.'[52] With that the men-at-arms arrived and dragged the clerks towards the fire. They threw them in with great fury, and in that way they suffered their martyrdom on the thirteenth day of November, for love of the good creator who never forgets his faithful servants. He is always ready to help them, for in their life and in their death his support never fails them. Blessed is he who serves him well, for this service is never in vain.[53] (1137–58)

Lords, you have heard very clearly how these martyrs met their end. Their suffering ended in death and thereby they gained true life. Through this death they escaped the eternal death in which they lived before. For if they had not put their belief in

God, they would all have been eternally lost. But the good lord did not wish them to have to perish in that way. Through his grace, which encompasses everything, he drew them to him in his mercy.[54] (1159–70)

I wish to recount a miracle which God deigned to perform on their behalf. Those who were thrown into the fire and had lain there for a long time were not in the slightest injured or consumed by the flame, nor was their fine colour spoilt or their clothing damaged. The good Jesus so protected them that not a single hair on their head was harmed. Their complexions appeared so fresh that you would not have realized they were dead. Such a lord is deserving of love who can so honour his own.[55] He feeds the souls in heaven above and honours the bodies here below. He feeds them there by his presence and preserves their bodies here by his power. His mercy is very great and his goodness ineffable, since he maintains his friends in this way and draws his enemies to him. Whoever hates him he loves dearly, and anyone who flees him he calls back. Oh, how gentle he is and how good, since he never fails his own! He governs everything, and everything is his, for he alone is good in all ways. Everything he has created is good, for all things experience his goodness. He never created anything without its experiencing his excellence. All things were created good, no matter how they have since changed. God never created anything bad, and it would be great folly to dare to say that individuals are pre-destined to sin against their will, or that they are forced to do evil in spite of a wish to avoid it. Everyone ought to blame themselves for the evil they do and thank God for the good. For it is from him alone that our good comes; he alone can curb evil. He binds evil and destroys it, and his great goodness is experienced by all. These clerks experienced his goodness when they converted to him; they came to scorn him, and he made them convert to him. He loved them; they hated him. He pursued them; they fled from him. He reached them with his goodness and brought them back to the rightful truth. Through death he called them to life, and with his help they won it indeed. Through death they had to seek life, and through their battle they won peace.[56] The good God who deigned to save them did not wish to forget their bodies. He rewarded their souls and kept their bodies from the flames. They remained whole and beautiful; the flame was never able to touch them. Many who saw this miracle converted to God's law. The Christians removed the bodies by night and buried them all. (1171–1238)

The tyrant saw what was happening and he found it extremely distressing and hard to bear. The shame he had undergone filled him with anguish, but when he saw that nothing could be done, he turned towards the maiden. He addressed her with these words: 'Oh, fair maiden, how lovely your face is. Those eyes are so well set; they always seem to have a wise smile in them. No mortal woman born on this earth can be compared to you in beauty. A mantle of royal purple would be very fitting for that beautiful body. Now consider your youth and follow our true path. It would certainly make me very happy if you would believe me. I suffer greatly on your account, fair one, since you scorn our law and consider our gods false and worthless and full of the enemy's cunning. Fair friend, leave this be, for you have good reason to fear that they may take vengeance on you; they are very merciful in their patience.[57] If you were to take my advice, you would sacrifice to our gods. You will certainly have great honour from doing so. You will be in second place in my palace, and together with the queen you will possess all my realm, except for her dowry, for I do not wish to wrong her in that regard. No distinction will be made between you except for the bed in which she will lie.[58] Those whom you wish to honour in court will truly be able to boast of honour and no one will be able to elevate those whom you wish to abase. I shall do even more for you if you will do what I wish. I shall have an image cast and have it honoured in your name. It will stand in the middle of my palace and hold a beautiful sceptre in its hand; all those who see it will greet it with humility. If there is anyone so bold as to pass by without a salutation, he will be considered as guilty as anyone who desired to harm me. No one will have committed a crime so great that it cannot be immediately pardoned if he has bowed low to this image and cried to it for mercy. I shall do you still greater honour, so that no one could do greater. In addition to my other promises, among the temples built for the goddesses I shall make one of marble in your name;

no one will ever have seen one richer.' This he said and a good deal more besides. (1239–1301)

The lady heard what he said and smiled. Very politely she said to him, by way of a witty little joke: 'Oh, how fortunate I am, since I am to be turned into gold! I'll have a statue in my name, and people will humbly venerate me. I shall be cast entirely in gold and adored like a goddess. It will suit me quite well, even if it is made of silver. If it is of a baser metal, upon my word, there is no harm in that. Whatever the metal it is cast in, I shall be hugely honoured by it, and you will be able to cast a body for it but without being able to give it life. Now tell me, if you can, the source and nature of the matter which makes mortal bodies live and gives them sight and hearing, so that they can speak and hear, walk, see and feel. If my statue does not possess such capabilities, its body will certainly be of little value. Its wisdom will be of little use to it since it cannot hear or speak. Now you will perhaps reply that this statue, which will be made in my name and worshipped by your followers, will bring me great glory. Oh, what honour they will do me when they speak such praise of me as "This is Catherine who abandoned her God and her faith". King, I do not care for such honour, for praise like that is really blame. Emperor, as long as you live, you will be able to force your men to do this honour to me, either from fear or love of you, but tell me what the birds which fly over me will do? Will they spare me on your account, so as not to alight on me? In no time at all they will have pecked out my eyes and sullied my shining face. Even your dogs will abuse me. Such, king, is your praise. Therefore, I say to you, emperor, that you should abandon your error, for it is worldly glory and folly. Anyone who believes this is certainly very foolish. I shall not believe you, now or ever, so you labour in vain. For Jesus Christ, my bridegroom, so desires my love that the two of us have already made a covenant that I am his beloved and he is my lover. He is my renown and my honour; he is my glory and my worth. He is my pleasure and my comfort, my sweetness and my delight. I love him so much that I cannot be parted from him; for I love him alone, and him alone do I desire. I am fully aware that he loves me in return and I for my part love him with such faith that I shall never abandon him for anything which anyone may say to me.' (1302–70)

This she said to him, and a good deal more than you have heard here, for she wanted to test him, by preaching and by entreaty, to see if she could yet rescue him from evil, so that he might want to do good. But, however much one may test an evil-doer, one will find nothing but evil in him; the more eloquently one entreats him, the more his wickedness increases. This is the effect she had on the evil tyrant about whom I have been speaking to you; wickedness gained ground in his heart from the good which he heard, and which he did not like.[59] Then he said to her very deceitfully: 'Fair one, watch out for your life. You have seriously dishonoured me by refusing my offer. You will have to sacrifice to the gods and ask for mercy with humility, or else I shall soon allow myself to be persuaded to cut off your fair head. But first I shall have you so beaten and battered that you will not know which way to turn.' (1371–94)

She replied with a laugh: 'I desire and request this. I ought to suffer pain readily for him, since he deigned to die for me. If necessary I shall suffer death, for he did so undeservedly on my behalf. For my sake he was taken and bound, beaten and battered. He endured great pain and hardship: I shall never be able to suffer as much for him. If I experience pain and suffering for his sake, this is joy and great sweetness to me. You will never be able to plan so much torment that I shall not wish to bear more. The day will come, and it is near at hand, when you yourself will suffer a great deal of pain, for, as I believe, the enemy will have the same power over you as God has lent you over his people, and a good deal more. For our pain is transitory, but yours will be eternal; in return for this earthly pain we shall have supreme glory. I know well that your aim is to kill me alone. But I shall tell you one thing: I shall not be going alone to God. Through your wrongdoing you have already sent many people to him from this palace, people whose bodies you have killed but who now live in paradise.' (1395–1426)

With this she fell silent. He became very angry and deep down in his heart sighed heavily. Then he ordered her to be taken and thrown into a dark dungeon. But before she was placed in the dungeon he had her beaten with leaded whips. Whilst blows were raining down on her from those who were taking her there, she cried out joyfully to the tyrant: 'I accept this torment willingly in the name of Jesus Christ, my beloved, who suffered death for me on the cross. He submitted his body to cruel scourges for the sake of me whom he saved in his goodness. When he took our humanity, he placed himself in a narrow dungeon. He whom the whole world cannot contain lay for a long time in a womb. But he encompasses in himself the entire world and all creatures within it. He who lavishes his grace on others lay in that confinement for my sake, and for love of him I shall gladly accept the darkness of this dungeon which I see here, for he did much more for me. I must tell you that in return for this darkness such light will be given to me that no tempest or chill wind will ever dim it. (1427–56)

Then the evil tyrant ordered the soldiers to take her, beat her with iron rods and put her in the dungeon. They did his bidding and beat her very savagely, wounding her tender body so brutally that the blood flowed out from every part. She was not in the least terrified by this, but gave praise to God. Again and again the tyrant said to her: 'Come now, do as I command and you will have relief from this torment, which is causing your whole body to bleed.'[60] 'You cowardly dog,' said the maiden, 'do whatever your evil heart predisposes you to do. You will never be able to do me so much harm that it will ever change my mind. Since he wanted to save me through pain, it is fitting that through pain I come to him.' Then he ordered them to stop the beating and put her at once in the dungeon, where she was to be left for twelve days without food or water. The lady was immediately seized and placed in a stinking dungeon. But the good lord, who is never far from his faithful and for whose love she endured this suffering, came to her aid there at this time of need. His angels visited her and gently comforted her, descending with such brightness that the warders were astonished. But they said nothing to the tyrant, as they feared his cruelty. (1457–92)

One day, it happened that the Emperor Maxentius had travelled some distance on business, which would keep him away for some time. In his palace was the queen, who had heard how her lord had treated the maiden, how she was shut in the dungeon on account of the great humiliation he had suffered in respect of the clerks whom she had vanquished so thoroughly, and how they had suffered for believing in God. She had also heard of the miracle whereby fire could not blemish them.[61] She felt great pity for the maiden, for she was told that she was very beautiful, and she felt compassion for her youth, as it was now the thireenth day that she had been shut in the dungeon without anything to eat or drink. The queen was very disturbed that such youth should perish in that way. She would have liked to visit her, but did not know how she could manage to do so. While she was suffering this anguish and wondering what to do about her, she made her way towards the palace and met Lord Porphiry. He was a prince of high lineage, loyal and noble of heart. A worthy man amongst the pagans, he behaved towards everyone with good faith. The lady addressed him, saying: 'Porphiry, fair friend, I wish to tell you what is on my mind, but I beg you, in God's name, to keep it secret. I have dreamt a strange dream and have been greatly disturbed by it. Do you know that girl whom my lord scourges so? In the night I dreamt that I saw her in a house where I was. I saw her set in such brightness that I could only just make her out. I saw two lords sitting with her and I have never set eyes on more regal people. They had such radiant faces that I did not dare look at them. Seeing me, she called me and commanded me to draw near. She took hold of a crown held by one of the people sitting with her, and calling me "empress" in kindly fashion placed it on my head. Then she said to me graciously: "Jesus Christ sends this to you." Since having this dream, I have not been able to rest or sleep. Instead, I am so disturbed that I can think of nothing else. All my desire is centred on one thing, that I might be able to see her and hear her. Friend, if I do not have your co-operation, I do not see how this could happen.' (1493–1556)

'Lady', he said, 'my will and my assistance are at your command. You must let me know what you want and I shall carry it out as your servant. I shall do all I can to accomplish your will. Even though my lord may hate me for it, I shall not desist from carrying out this task on that account. But I shall tell you the marvel which I have seen concerning her. I saw her debating with the clerks and refuting their arguments in such a way that alone she defeated fifty clerks, who were expert debaters. They were all then converted to belief in her God and suffered martyrdom for him. Lady, the king, your lord, felt so distressed by this that he had them all thrown into the fire. But the fire failed to harm them. Nevertheless, they all lost their lives, and people said that they went to heaven. Since I first saw this lady I have been so shaken that I certainly hold it utter folly that anyone should sacrifice to our gods. There is nothing for it but to consider how we can get to speak with her. I shall win over her gaolers with money, so that they will do what we want.' When he had said this, he departed. He made a bargain with the guards, who agreed to give them the freedom to carry out their wishes. (1557–90)

During the first watch of the night, the two of them set out towards the dungeon, without any escort. They finally reached it and fell to the ground in fear, because of the great brightness they saw there. But then they became aware of a sweet smell, which restored their strength. The maiden raised them up and comforted them gently. They saw angels come down to heal her tender body, for she was wounded all over by the harsh blows from the scourges. Presently she called the empress and placed a very fine crown of gold on her head. Then she turned her face in the other direction. 'My lords,' she said, 'this is the lady about whom I made my entreaty to God, that he might make her my companion and put her on the path of true faith. I also wish to pray to him that he give this knight a proper understanding of what is right and make him a companion of mine.' (1591–1616)

They said to God's beloved: 'God has heard your prayer. You will be readily listened to, whatever you ask of him. Those who have come here for your sake will be converted to a belief in him, so that they will suffer death for him and have eternal life. When you have won your battle, the merciful Jesus will receive you and place you in paradise, where you will always see his shining face. You will dwell there with your bridegroom, whose glory continues for ever.'[62] (1617–30)

Then she turned towards the queen and reassured her gently. 'Queen,' she said, 'fair friend, my lord invites you to his nuptials. Be a lady of high courage and fear no earthly torment, for pain here and great worldly sorrow are as nothing compared with the joy of paradise, which God promises to those who love him. Do not fear the emperor; desire his love no longer. His love is weak and deceptive and his power ephemeral. He is so unsure about his own life. If he is alive today, he does not know whether he will be alive tomorrow. If he is resplendent in purple today, he does not know if tomorrow he will be food for maggots. Such a one is called king in the evening and on the following day is buried. Such is human power; there is no certain joy in it. My lady queen, for this reason I beg you not to fear this mortal husband. You must not fear his power, or even desire his love. But place all your desire in him who can condemn or save you, and who in exchange for these transient pains will give us everlasting joys.' (1631–60)

With that Lord Porphiry addressed her, saying: 'Lady, what is it that God gives to those who suffer death for him? Can they have any consolation afterwards?' She answered him readily: 'Friend Porphiry, listen to me. Do you see how changeable this world is and that nothing in it is stable?[63] There will never be anyone so rich that he cannot lose his wealth. The life of a man is soon over; however long his life is, it is still brief. No one will live for so long that it will not seem a short time when he feels the approach of death. If in his life he had great honour, so much greater will be his sorrow. The world's success turns to loss and its wealth to great poverty. Even worldly happiness is a great sorrow to those who have it. Man gains honour with difficulty and loses it with great sadness. There is no one so knowledgeable or wise as to be able to escape the world's harm. When things turn out this way, I see no one who does not end up complaining. Friend, you can understand this if you give it a little thought. It is not only to men that this world affords shame and torment. Consider these great cities and how they have lost their grandeur. You are well aware of how they have altered since their foundation. The world and everything in it goes from bad to worse. (1661–96)

Friend, you asked just now what gift God will give to his saints. It will be the gift of eternal life, which will never be destroyed by death. Once one has gained it, it will never afterwards be lost. Since man strives for this life, which is never secure in itself, how intensely ought everyone to labour to gain that life which is full of sweetness and does not fear death or suffering. I shall tell you what the country is like which God promises to his friends. It is a bright city which has no need of any other light. In it no one is far from what he needs; no one there lacks for anything. There is never any adversity or tribulation. No hardship or sorrow is to be found there, nor any pride, envy or folly. Nor is there any lamenting or weeping or foolish longings, nor any covetousness or false witness.[64] There old age is not scorned, and no foolhardiness or idleness exists there. Misfortune does not befall those who are there, for their joy is sure. So great and so perfect is their joy that it pleases them equally all the time. There is comfort there for sorrow, and joyful gladness to combat vexation. The life which destroys death is there and the day which does not await the night. Charity dwells there and honour, abundance, generosity and worth. Nobility is there and felicity, magnificence and great humility.[65] Everything which dwells there is good; no evil thing can reach that place. (1697–1736)

In this great royal city there dwells at all times the immortal king, who had no beginning and will have no end, a king who is beautiful, merciful, glorious and the delight of chaste lovers.[66] His power is felt by everything, earth, sea and all that belongs to them. There too is the beautiful queen, who is both mother and maiden. Within her chaste body she bore her good maker who created her. He is her son and her father, and she is his daughter and his mother. From her blossomed the flower which feeds everything with its perfume. From her grew the good fruit by which hell has been destroyed. This lady is the blessed Mary; she is mother to the king who maintains life. Nature marvels at her, for there was never such a creature. She is a joy to the sorrowful, and the consolation of orphans. Our trust rests in her; she is our hope of life. She alone is the empress by whom the whole world is healed. She alone is the lady and queen before whom all things bow down. She has been taken up to paradise and sits crowned beside her son.[67] (1737–68) The great company of angels is there with their singing, the sweet festive song, which is unvaryingly magnificent. There also are the young men and the noble knights who, as holy martyrs, conquered death and suffered it for the love of God.[68] The apostles and the good doctors of the church are there, as well as the good confessors. There too is the choir of young women, virgins and chaste maidens who despised mortal lovers, choosing instead the chaste love of God. All praise in unison the name of the all-powerful king. Friend, what I have told you is a tiny amount of the inexpressible pleasure created by the joy of paradise, which God promises to his friends. But one thing I say to you for certain is that the eye cannot see nor the ear hear nor the heart ever imagine nor the tongue narrate the great joy which is there, and which God will give to his faithful.[69] Yet you will be able to know it, if you have a perfect desire for it.' (1769–96)

The empress and Lord Porphiry were full of joy at what they had heard. They felt great joy in their hearts as a result of the brightness they had seen. If it should please him, they were quite ready to suffer death for God. With that they left the dungeon, filled with joy and strength. Lord Porphiry was asked by his knights where he had been and he said to them: 'Do not ask me, but I beseech you to accept my advice. I shall tell you what happened to me during the holy watch which I kept. I have been shown knowledge of God and true belief in him. We shall all be lost at the end if we do not believe in this God. If you are willing to believe in him, you will have eternal life. The idols we worship here are the cult of the enemy, but this God is both king and lord, and so good that I do not know how to relate it all to you. Believe in his son Jesus Christ, who made all things from nothing. He gives life to his followers, which will not be destroyed through sorrow. He has shown us the true faith, through the imprisoned maiden whose name is Catherine. She has expounded the divine law to us.' The knights who heard this gladly believed in his God. There were two hundred and more there who believed in God's powers. They all abandoned their false religion in favour of the good God in whom they believed. (1797–1834)

The maiden was in the dungeon and she called her good lord to her aid. She had already been there for twelve days without tasting any food. But she had celestial food, which sustained her very well. A white dove, which God sent her from heaven, brought it to her. God himself appeared to her in the dungeon where she lay, and there was a vast company of angels who came in attendance. The choir of virgins followed him there as their bridegroom and lover.[70] Then the good lord comforted her; he called her his good daughter. 'Fair one,' he said, 'I am Jesus for whom you have endured so many ills. I am your maker who created you and for whom you have undertaken this battle. Do not fear, I am with you; you will not lack for my help. Through you many will come to believe in me and will dwell with me for ever.'[71] When Jesus Christ had said this to her, he went back to heaven and she remained behind. Before her eyes he ascended into heaven in such a way that she was able to watch him for a long time. (1835–62)

When he had completed his business, the tyrant set out on his return journey. He came back to Alexandria, to the city which he had left. That night he rested and next day he rose early and went to an upper chamber. Then he summoned his powerful barons. The lords and the provosts who maintained his religion and his honour came to him, and then the wicked tyrant ordered that the young woman be brought before him. She was quickly led from the dungeon and brought into his presence. Everyone stared at the maiden, amazed by her beauty. The emperor was greatly astonished that her face was so beautiful and bright, for he had hoped that fasting would destroy her beauty, thus enabling him to conquer her. So he commanded his gaolers to come to him and confess instantly who had given her food whilst she had been in the dungeon. (1863–88)

When she realized his cruel intentions towards the gaolers whom he had summoned she did not want them to be condemned and put to death on her account. 'King,' she said, 'in this matter you have proved that you rule this realm wrongfully. You ought rather to put right what is wrong and not condemn people for something good. You wrongly accuse your men-at-arms; it never occurred to them to give me food. Thanks be to God, I had no need of it. I want you to understand that at no time did I have any earthly food, for my bridegroom, my sweet lover, nourished me well in his mercy. He sent me a dove from heaven which brought me my food.' (1889–1906)

Then the tyrant replied with a benign, but false countenance: 'Oh,' he said, 'what great sorrow I have, fair one, at this error of yours, that so noble a king's daughter, and one so beautiful as I see you to be, should be shamefully besotted by the false art of sorcery. I have a great desire to see your foolish error corrected. I shall not hold you any longer, but now you will need your intelligence. You may choose between two things; mind you do not choose the worse. Worship our gods and you will live, or otherwise you will die shamefully. With the harsh torments which I shall have carried out on you, your tender body will be torn to pieces.' (1907–24)

She replied: 'I long to live in such a way that God may be my life. I am not afraid of suffering death for him, for I desire it with all my heart. You may well be able to kill my body, but you have no power over my soul, nor can you kill my body in such a way as to prevent it from rising again in the life beyond. Use against my body all the torments you can devise, for God calls me through martyrdom as his humble handmaiden. For my sake God made an offering of himself to his father: it is right that I should repay him for it. He offered his flesh and his blood for me, and through his own death turned my death back to life. For him I shall gladly die, and I know that in him I shall live again. I say to you that without fail the day of my vengeance is close at hand, when God will avenge me on you through a man of our faith.[72] He will have such power over you that he will cut off your head. Your wicked gods will be delighted with your accursed blood. They will make a sacrifice of you in the vileness of hell, where they will remain for ever. Yet, if you will only believe me, you may still turn aside from this path. So believe in God, who created you, and if you so desire, he will save you.' (1925–56)

When the tyrant understood that she was threatening him in this manner, he gnashed his teeth like a lion and scowled like a criminal. 'Ah,' he said, 'how shamed I am when I am so vilified by this woman. What makes me hesitate to have her torn limb from limb? Take her immediately and beat her for as long as she still lives. Then we shall see the great assistance she gets from her good God, in whom she trust so much.' (1957–68)

She was then immediately taken and subjected to this great torment. Many felt great compassion for her beauty and courage. They begged her to abandon her faith and obey the tyrant. 'Fair one,' they said, 'be mindful of yourself. You are too hard on your own youth. It is a matter of great sorrow and loss that you destroy your youthful self in this way. Take pity on your youth and abandon your foolish plans.' (1969–80)

'Lords,' she said, 'do not weep and do not lament for my beauty. It is no use your lamenting this beauty, which has no permanence. This beautiful, white and tender flesh will have to be given back to the earth. Earth it is and earth it will become, and to dust it will revert. Worms will devour it and reduce it to vile dust. Therefore, I say to you, do not weep for me, but, I beg you, take pity on yourselves. For you are without hope of life when this life is taken from you. My torments will pass, but yours will be eternal. This death gives me hope of life, but your death leads you to death. Your death takes you to death, but mine will be certain life.'[73] (1981–2000)

Many who heard what she said abandoned their religion and their idols; yet they kept this a secret because of the emperor, whom they feared. They did not wish it known, until they had heard and seen what would happen to the maiden in respect of the battle she had begun. (2001–8)

At that moment there came forward a man who was filled with the enemy's cunning. He was a provost in the palace, and his name was Cursates. Wanting to incite the wicked to wickedness, he exhorted the king to do evil. 'Alas,' he said, 'oh, mighty king, how amazed I am at you, whose power and wisdom have suffered this woman for so long without taking vengeance on her and punishing her. King, you are greatly dishonoured by all the resistance she has shown. But I can tell you that no torment has yet come near to frightening Catherine or even to dismaying her greatly. Trust me when I say now that I shall give you some advice which will make her sacrifice to the gods or deliver her to a cruel death. Now, within no longer than three days, have four wheels made and let the inner and outer rims be thickly studded with nails. On the connecting spokes of the wheels have a number of sharp, cutting blades placed close together. Then have her brought forward to me and placed beside the wheel. Let her then see how swiftly they turn, run and spin, and if she is willing to sacrifice to the gods, she will succeed in escaping death. If not, let her be taken immediately and placed amid the wheels. Her body will soon be dismembered and chopped up by the blades. I tell you this: the Christians who see this will be filled with terror.' (2009–50)

The king accepted what the man said. He ordered the wheels

to be made and they were quickly prepared and cruelly devised. The third day had hardly dawned when the emperor commanded the wheels to be brought to the pretorium in order to carry out his wickedness. His orders were obeyed and they were soon brought out. (2051–60)

I shall tell you as much as I know about the construction of the wheels.[74] There were four of them, large and broad, designed in such a way that they were covered with sharp nails all over the front and rear spokes. When two of the wheels rose up, the others moved down, and they met each other with such a velocity that nothing between them could survive. For the nails collided with the blades so that the blades sharpened the nails, with the result that there was nothing on earth so hard that it would not be completely cut to pieces and chopped into little morsels, if it were there for a single moment. The tyrant was delighted with this and he ordered her to be brought forward and placed among the wheels, if she did not immediately sacrifice to the gods. (2061–79)

The men-at-arms led her forward and showed her the great wheels; but she was not in the least dismayed, either by their threats or by the torment. To him who comforts all sorrows she turned for his gracious help. 'Oh, almighty king,' she said, 'you who have created everything from nothing, oh sweet, oh compassionate, oh merciful one, deliverer of all the wretched, listen, lord, to this wretched woman, who fights for you amidst torment, and destroy this wicked device with swift thunderbolts and fire. By your grace, lord, bring this about so that your holy name may be praised. Lord, you know my thoughts well; I do not do this to escape death, for I am not afraid to die for you; rather do I desire it with all my heart. My body will gladly suffer whatever torment is pleasing to you.' (2080–2102)

When the lady had finished speaking, an angel came down from heaven. He began to whirl the wheels round so that not a spoke remained intact. He swung them with such violence that not a single joint could hold. He sent them flying among the assembled ranks, killing four thousand of those who were there to mock God's might. Then sorrow grew among the pagans, and joy and gladness among the Christians. The noise was great, the cries loud, and the tyrant was greatly distressed by it. In his heart he felt great anguish and he did not know what on earth he could do. At that moment the queen suddenly arrived. Wanting to see the maiden, she had gone up into a tower and had heard the cries from this great slaughter. She came down from the tower immediately and, seeing the opportunity to declare herself, did not want to stay hidden any longer. She addressed him fiercely, saying: 'Oh, wretched lord, if you intend to struggle against God, it is not strength that you need. It is only too obvious that you are acting disloyally by making war on your own creator. Do you expect to be successful in this war which you have waged against his servants and handmaidens whom you have so cruelly scourged? Now God, who killed so many thousands of men with the thunderbolt he sent down, has clearly shown you how great is his power. He burnt the wheels you had made; you have gained nothing but shame and frustration.' At these words there arrived many pagans, who had seen the miracle which God wrought there: the thunderbolt he sent from heaven, the wheels which had been burnt there and the men who died. They began to cry out and to praise the might of God: 'This God in whom the Christians believe is king and all-powerful. We shall henceforth believe in him, for he alone is God: this we know very well.' (2103–54)

When the king heard these words, he nearly went mad with rage. Then in his fury he wondered how he could do them the greatest possible harm. He would have them all killed together with savage torment and suffering, and afterwards he would certainly plan more torments for the queen than for the others. Then he turned towards her, for she caused him to have great sorrow in his heart: 'Queen,' he said, 'how is it that you challenge what is right? The Christians have practised sorcery on you, for you are completely bewitched. I have lost all my honour now that they have misled you so. Queen, where shall I find comfort after your painful death? I cannot avoid having you put to death, but thereafter my life will be a living death. How will you live without me and how shall I live without you? You were my sole reason for desiring good fortune and it is for your sake that I used to fear misfortune and avoid it. But I have indeed avoided it badly, since I have encountered it at your hands. Alas, what good is my love to me now when I receive nothing from it but pain? I shall live out my life in great sadness once I have lost you, my fair friend. For you alone were my delight and I yours, I believe. But now I know and understand very well that presumption often damages us. Because I loved you so much, I assumed the same of you, but now you have proved to me that this was nothing but presumption. Now I am wretched, completely misled, slain, betrayed and confounded. I shall never again have any comfort and now I desire nothing but death. I shall never be able to recover from losing what I most desired, and when I have lost the greater part, can I be sustained by the lesser? My power will be of little use to me when I have lost what I want. For if I cannot have what I want, what do I care for what I do not want? What joy can I have from power which contradicts desire? Wretch that I am, I can do everything I do not want, and that which I want most I cannot do. I amass power counter to my desire, but I lament this powerless desire. For if I had power to effect my desire, my trouble would be ended. Now I do not know what to aim for, when I cannot realize my desire, or to what concerns my heart should turn when all honour flees from me. I shall be much despised and the least feared of all my people, when my wife shames me in this way and abandons me on account of such folly, I who am king and emperor of this realm, charged with punishing the Christians and forcing them to abandon their foolishness! Now they have so duped my people as to cause them to hold all my gods in contempt. What counsel can I take over the loss of my wife?[75] If our mutual love so constrains me that I take no vengeance on this folly, what will these other noble ladies do? Upon my word, they will take their precedent from her and deceive their husbands into believing these heresies. One must choose the lesser of two evils. It is more fitting that I exercise justice than that my whole realm should be destroyed because of her folly. I prefer to act against my heart's desires rather than that everyone should come to harm because of me. Lady,' he said, 'I tell you, and rather than threaten you, I beg you to abandon this folly to which you have so miserably succumbed. For, if you do not, I shall kill you, as I know no better counsel. But you will certainly not have the pleasure of knowing that your torment will be ended by the sentence of death, for I shall deprive you of the comfort of a quick death. For you I can devise new torments; I shall tear your breasts from your body before I give you leave to die and allow you to enjoy your death.'[76] (2155-2256)

Then he ordered them to take her and carry out these torments on her. At the moment when those obeying the wicked tyrant seized her, the lady glanced around and, seeing the virgin, called to her, saying: 'Oh, royal maid, offer prayers for this handmaiden of the lord to your great God, who is so good and who provides complete reassurance for his own.[77] For love of him I have abandoned my faith and embraced this suffering. Pray that he may have mercy on me and so implant his faith in my heart that this frail and miserable flesh, which always struggles against everything good, does not deprive me of the crown which God gives to his knights.' The maiden said to her: 'Fair friend, do not be at all afraid, but conduct yourself nobly,[78] for today you will receive, in exchange for this short and frail life, the great joy which knows no end. You will receive birth through death, so that you can die no more. In place of the one you have forsaken, you will receive a lover whose beauty illuminates the world and who is king over everyone. For this vain and desolate empire you will receive a sure kingdom into which no suffering has ever entered. Everything there is joy, for the king who sustains it is gentle. Everything which reaches there becomes sweet. Everything is sweetened with the sweetness which derives from him. Nothing has strength to resist this sweetness.'[79] (2257-96)

When the queen heard this, she gathered such courage and took so much comfort in God that she willingly exhorted the men-at-arms to delay no longer in carrying out the tyrant's will. Then they led her outside the city and put a great deal of effort into torturing her. With nails of sharpened steel, they pierced her breasts, which were very soft and beautiful. Then they tore them out of her chest. They used these nails to hang her up and they cut off her beautiful head. So the queen died as a result of the maiden's exhortation. Her sorrow was ended by torture on the twenty-third day of November.[80] She died on a Wednesday; she lost life and found life. Lord Porphiry, about whom I told you earlier, and who was a very great friend to her,[81] took with him some of his knights and his closest advisers. They removed her body by night, and anointed and embalmed it well. They buried it with great honour, but in great secrecy, for the tyrant had commanded that her body should remain unburied, her flesh being given over to the birds and devoured by wild animals. But this had not deterred them from burying her. (2297–2330)

When the day dawned, the king arose and dressed. He was very troubled and distressed and his entire household was grief-stricken. Sorrow was neighbour to them all on account of their love for the good queen. Knights and men-at-arms wept, as did people old and young. Pages and squires wept, and everywhere there was great sorrow. Both in the town and the castle young knights and young noblemen wept. Townsmen and peasants displayed great grief. In chambers and stone halls, ladies and maidens wept. You should have seen these maidens as they went in search of their lady, whom they had lost. They did not know what had become of her. Certainly, anyone who has ever loved a woman would feel compassion. The king himself was greatly distressed by the fact that the body had been removed.[82] He began to make enquiries amongst those of his men whom he suspected. (2331–56)

Porphiry heard of his cruelty towards his men whom he had accused. He had no desire to remain concealed any longer. Instead he went forward and addressed the king: 'King,' he said, 'what are you thinking of? Demons have driven you crazy. You are behaving contrary to reason and with false religion. I can see you blaming your men here for something for which you ought to be championing them. You should be very grateful to them if they have buried her body. Whoever heard tell of such a body being given over to beasts? Who could hate another person so much that he would not agree to a lowly sepulchre of earth for their body? You demonstrate your evil nature in having denied so much as a little earth to the woman you loved so greatly. If you dare accuse me of it, I am the one who did it; I shall not hide it from you. I am the one who took her body away and buried it with great honour. If you are going to condemn anyone for this, I alone should stand accused.' (2357–82)

Now there was much sorrow and grief when the king heard that his close friend had opposed him so stoutly. He roared aloud like a madman and threw himself down, crying: 'Wretch that I am, what is my life worth? My mother bore me in an evil hour; I am a slave, not an emperor, for nothing of mine is left which the Christians do not take away from me. They have taken away and misled the very best members of my kingdom. Everyone ought to feel pity for me since my own people deceive me in this way. Porphiry, whom I loved so much and in whom I trusted above all men, was the guardian of my life, my comfort and my helper. I have never been so angry that he could not fill me with joy. He took charge of all my great undertakings and supported all my concerns. Now I do not know why he has become so dreadfully foolish that he scorns my gods and my faith. But I do know and believe one thing, that he misled my wife, for he was her counsellor. Wretch that I am, I see that this harm can never be undone. So it is not right for me to lament. Let us forget what cannot be, but what I believe I can recover I ought to mourn in order to correct it. One often sees people who complain getting what they want. I should not hold back my complaint if I could achieve my will thereby. Now there is only one course of action. I must behave as everyone does. One ought to choose the lesser of two evils. Therefore I must take vengeance for my injury and shame, for complaining is of no avail.[83] But, if he wished to repent and agree to what I wanted, that would be in accord with my wishes, for I greatly desire him to make amends.' (2383–2430)

Then he summoned the two hundred knights of whom I spoke earlier. With false words of friendship, he complained of their lord to them, but they all asserted unanimously that they believed in Jesus Christ. Then he ordered them to be tortured, beaten, reviled and humiliated. When Lord Porphiry saw that they were being so harshly treated, he feared they might change their minds on account of the torment. 'King,' he said, 'What do you mean by torturing them without me? If they have done wrong, I shall undertake their defence. I am their prince and their lord, and I made them abandon their folly. Your efforts are indeed in vain if you do not take vengeance on me.' (2431–50)

'Ah, friend Porphiry', said the king, 'since you are their leader and their lord, you ought to set them an example and get them to abandon their folly. Otherwise yours will be the first neck to be privy to the sword.' When he saw that they were quite unmoved, he immediately ordered them to be taken outside the city and all beheaded together and the bodies afterwards left for the dogs and not a single one of them buried. (2451–62)

Everything the king commanded was soon carried out on the twenty-fourth day of the month. On a Thursday they were killed for the glory of paradise;[84] may God allow us to reign with them in the place where he lives and reigns without equal. (2463–8)

In the morning the king rose, still unsatiated by the evil he had done and the martyrs he had killed. He had the maiden summoned and she was quickly brought to him. 'Now, my fair one', he said, 'I know very well that I lost my wife through you. You misled her and the others so that they have been put to death. Having caused this great harm, you will be wise to repent it. You can have great benefits if you will renounce your folly. You can be so fortunate as to have me for your spouse, or, if not, I assure you and swear to you by my gods and my faith that I shall have you killed in as foul a way as I know how, so that all those who see you will be grief-stricken by the mere sight of it.' (2469–90)

She said to him: 'Is it not a fact that man must suffer in exchange for joy? Such a death, by which one can obtain life, is not at all to be deplored. This death will be a birth for me, so that afterwards I shall have no fear of death. This pain will bring great joy to me, and this humiliation great honour. I assure you that I seek no obstacle to it. Do whatever you want, for you will find me ready for everything. I desire my bride-groom so much that to suffer pain will be sweet to me.' (2491–2504)

When he heard the way she had spoken, he became almost insane with rage. He ordered her to be taken away from him and led outside the town to be beheaded. She was taken there swiftly and nothing would have made anyone who witnessed this sadness seek one greater. There, many a face was wet with tears, and many a voice cried aloud. Many a fair eye was moist and many breathed a sigh of pity. Everyone, old and young, lamented, and this pursuit was common to all. The rich lamented her nobility, and the poor her generosity; the high-born lamented her lineage, and the common people lamented her misfortune. The ladies bemoaned her beauty, her intelligence and her good breeding. You should have seen these noble maidens weeping and beating their breasts! They lamented the fair Catherine as their companion and their neighbour. But most of all they lamented her youthful beauty.[85] But she could not be dissuaded for the sake of any companion or friend. She looked around her and saw the people following her. Seeing the ladies weep, she began to comfort them: 'Alas,' she said, 'noble maidens, and you, fair and noble baronesses, do not, I beg you in God's name, weep for me or have pity for my death.[86] If this is true pity, charity or affection, rejoice with me, for my good king is now summoning me, my bridegroom, my beloved, in whom I trust above all things. Turn to your own account these tears which you are wasting on me, I beg you, so that God may snatch you from this error before you reach the day of judgement.' (2505-50)

When God's beloved had said this, she humbly begged the man-at-arms to give her time to pray. Having no wish to deny her, he granted her this. She prostrated herself on the ground and then commenced her prayer. Holding her beautiful hands towards the heavens she said: 'Oh, omnipotent king, true sweetness, true salvation, sweet, merciful, good Jesus, my solace, my strength, my hope, my honour, I praise you, fair lord, for having provided me with this martyrdom and for calling me through this swift death to be numbered among your handmaidens. Lord, I beseech you, on behalf of all those who will need my help, and who for your sake will love me so much that they will seek your help through me, give them, lord, good help in their life and in their death and when they have pain or grief, so that through your grace I may be able to help them. Keep them, lord, from adversity and from severe illness and from plague and famine, and provide them with fair winds. Lord, give them plenty in their herds, their fruit and their wheat. And on me, fair lord, as I await the blow of the executioner here, I beseech you to have mercy at this time, so that you will deign to receive my soul, for this he cannot take away from you. I pray that it may be delivered to your angels and brought before your countenance, so that I may dwell with the virgins and praise your holy name for ever.' (2551-90)

She had barely finished her prayer when a voice of great resonance, issuing from the clouds, replied to her with these words: 'Come to me, fair beloved, come, come, my handmaiden. Your beloved has opened the great gate of paradise to you: your seat is raised up in the house of blessedness. The choir of virgins awaits you, together with all my faithful. They are all coming forth to meet you and rejoicing at your coming. I have willingly granted the boon you have asked of me. All those who commemorate you here will be received by me there in glory. In their pain and sorrow I shall be swift to succour them.' (2591–2610)

When the lady heard this voice, she stretched out her white neck to the sword. 'Friend,' she said to the grim sergeant, 'do the will of the tyrant. Do not be slothful, for my bridegroom summons me.' He jumped and raised the sword. Swiftly he beheaded her. (2611–18)

After this great sorrow, God wrought on that day two miracles which are worthy of remembrance. For this reason I do not wish to conceal them.[87] Her blood lost its ordinary nature, for it flowed there as white milk from her body. The other miracle God performed was that he sent to her his angels from heaven. They bore her body away with them and laid it on Mount Sinai. They placed it there with great honour. It lies there to this day, where God has performed many a miracle and does and will do for all our age. From the tomb where she lies, oil flows even now.[88] By this oil many are cured of their illness, to the praise of the creator for whom she suffered mortal pain. I shall return to her death, however, for I shall now tell you about her feast.[89] It was on the twenty-fifth day of November that her beautiful, tender body suffered death. She suffered death on a Friday at the hour at which God suffered it, for by his death he has saved us, if we desire it.[90] We are perfectly capable of having God, if we truly desire.[91] He has given us every opportunity to manifest our goodwill, for he so greatly desired our love that he created everything for us. He himself became a created being, through his bounty, not through his nature. He suffered death for our love, and torment, shame and great adversity. Oh, how we ought to praise him, to hold him dear against all evils, to desire his love and eschew all worldly love, when he, who alone is king and lord, so desires our love. How greatly a man would be loved if he had created at this moment such a heaven; and if he could fill it with so many stars, could form both land and sea and separate night from day, he would be greatly renowned. No one, should he be able to do this, could put in such a great amount of effort without being highly praised for it, as well as desired and greatly loved. Certainly, many people to whom he would never have given any particular benefit would love him, but God will never be loved by anyone who has not felt his goodness. No one loves him as he ought to be loved or in accordance with what he deserves. The love he has shown to us will never be repaid, but this lady loved him well and with her love rewarded him as far as she had the power to do so; no part of her will remained unexpressed.[91] (2619–84)

Now let us pray that by her goodness she will obtain for us the will to love God and to serve him and come to a happy end. Amen. (2685–8)

I who have translated her life am called Clemence by name. I am a nun of Barking, for love of which I took this work in hand.[92] For the love of God, I pray and beseech all who will hear this book and who listen to it with a receptive heart to pray to God on my behalf, that he may place my soul in paradise and guard my body while it is alive, he who reigns and lives and will reign, and is and was and will always be. (2689–2700)

Master, address yourself to this need and help me as your disciple.[1] Remember the words written by Jesus, son of Sirach: a true friend will never be put to a test at a time of prosperity.[2] But it is when someone needs him that he can test his friend, for at a time of need the friend will not remain hidden. Nor will an enemy remain hidden during adversity, for when he sees someone undergoing a period of suffering, he gives him a push downwards. A friend shows himself at a time of need, and an enemy hides from suffering. Show yourself at this time; when I have made errors, correct me.[3] A wiser person than I can make a mistake in a lesser matter than the treatment of such martyrdom. When I give thought to it, I become aware that we shall be here for a short time only and I do not know what burdens the world will impose upon us.[4] This life is only a shadow which deceives us and draws us towards death. Everyone dies, even the fierce and the strong. Life is short and the world is changeable; glory and suffering are permanent. Each of us should avoid the suffering and be drawn towards the sovereign glory. Ecclesiastes, son of David, said, when he described vanity, that everything perishes, nothing is renewed and no one finds a source of renewal.[5] No one can have riches unless someone else has had them. No one now has such great riches, knowledge, beauty or prowess that someone else has not had more. Oh God! What has become of Aristotle's great wisdom, Lord Caesar's riches, Samson's fame and strength and Absalom's great beauty?[6] What is the value of desire? Or of the will? Wherein lies the value of any delight one can have? Wherein that of the joy of this world? All delights come to nothing. Everything comes from nothing and reverts to nothing. He who takes too much wastes his time. He who sets his heart on wealth is a fool, for everyone dies, poor and rich; the wise man dies and so does the fool. However long it takes, they come to the same end, and they all go by a single route. In this world I see nothing durable except for the good which each of us can do (for which one may have mercy after one's death), or else the praise or fame for some piece of work which outlives one in this world. For this reason I am beginning such a work for you and request that it should be made available to everyone; it is about the passion and the torments which St Lawrence suffered for God, how he was punished for love of him and brought to martyrdom. Now let us pray to God that in his love, as he suffered pain for him, he will permit us to perform such deeds as will free our souls from pain. May his grace descend amongst us and protect us from affliction by the devil's treacherous devices, and may he give us everlasting joy in the kingdom of his majesty, where he lives and reigns in Trinity. (1-74)

I am composing this work, which I am beginning here, for a handmaiden of St Lawrence, who wants the story of him and his passion in order to keep him in her memory and to take his deeds as an example.[7] Anyone who is willing to listen to it with an open heart can thereby easily avoid folly. And if he wishes to act in God's service, God in his great glory will receive him, as we read in the story of the blessed and worthy Sixtus. When he was pope in Rome, the world was largely pagan and men were addicted to wrong-doing. The devil in his greed envied the holy church, and through those over whom he exercised power destroyed its members everywhere. (75-92)

Sixtus heard it said that a perfidious man was on his way to Rome.[8] His name was Decius Caesar and he was travelling through the region in order to get rid of Christianity.[9] He was making his way to the city of Rome. In his cruel greed he thought he could destroy the holy church, and as he wanted to frighten the others he intended to start with its head. For he who destroys the root renders the fruit of the branch of little value. He wanted to destroy the foundation, and St Sixtus was fully aware of this. In the headquarters of the bishopric Sixtus gathered together all his clergy in Rome. He comforted them and exhorted them to remember that they were close to the crown which Jesus had promised to his people in the kingdom of paradise, saying: 'Sons, be strong in God's name. Do not be afraid to suffer death for him, for he suffered for us. Let us in turn suffer for him in this way. Decius Caesar is descending upon us and soon he will take me away from you. You, who will be left behind after me, love God and keep his law!' (93-120)

Felicissimus and Agapitus, who were both deacons, said to him: 'Fair father, where will you be going without us? What will become of us without you?' Sixtus summoned St Lawrence,[10] who was from a good family. He was a deacon, a good cleric and a wealthy man. He was archdeacon of Rome,[11] and Sixtus told him to guard all the treasures so that Decius would have no share of them: 'I place the entire responsibility for them on you.' Lawrence replied: 'Where will you be going without me? Where are you going without your sons? Father, what shall I do? Take me with you! What am I to do here after you?' St Sixtus replied to him: 'Do not be sad at my departure. We shall be together by the third day. I am not abandoning you. You will follow me and be with me by the third day.'[12] There was a great miracle in these words, because in his own death he saw the other's death. He knew that he himself must die and he knew that St Lawrence would do so too.[13] (121-44)

St Lawrence understood prophetically that the end of his life was near. From the church he took the gold and all the silver, both in vessels and robes, everything he could find, and then went and sold it to the Christians.[14] He gathered all the poor together and gave them everything in God's name. He paid back God's blessing and understood the verse in the psalter which Lord David prophesied. He *distributed* things and gave everything to the poor.[15]* His justice endured for ever; he did not want the devil's disciples to have the property of the holy church. He performed an act of reasonable justice in giving away for the love of God the property which was entrusted to him. For, if it had been discovered in his possession, he would not have retained it for God's use. He spent it all on the followers of God, and they ate and drank.[16] He was well aware that nevertheless the tyrants would ill-treat him as a result of this.[17] (145-68)

Decius and the entire senate went to where the clerics were gathered and said: 'Sixtus, do you know why we have come

here?'[18] Sixtus replied: 'Yes, very well!' 'Come with us then,'
said Decius, 'make sacrifice to our gods or otherwise you will
die.' Sixtus replied: 'Sacrifice to them? I shall sacrifice to God
for evermore. I shall not make sacrifice to your gods out of fear
or greed, for they understand nothing and are mute. Whatever
one does for them is lost. Are they not made of gold and of
silver?'[19] When Decius heard this, he broke out into a sweat
from anger and spite. Nevertheless, he began with these words:
'Think hard, change your mind. Take pity on your age, lest you
die through your foolishness.[20] Do not lead your followers into
error or let them have a bad example in you. Be aware that if
you abandon your faith I shall provide you with great wealth
and raise you above your people.' Sixtus said: 'I have made my
decision and I reject your gods and renounce your laws. I believe
wholeheartedly in God, and in view of my advanced years I
must serve God all the more and maintain his faith against
everyone, so that no one can say afterwards that in my old age I
abandoned my faith.' (169–202)

When Decius heard this, he commanded his men to take him
to the temple of Mars.[21] He ordered his head to be cut off if he
refused to worship his god. Then the knights took him to the
statue in the temple of Mars, and St Sixtus said fiercely: 'Statue,
you who cannot hear or see, you who deceive foolish people,
may you be destroyed and confounded!' Then a large part of
the dreadful temple of Mars fell down, and Decius Caesar's
knights were greatly angered by this and they led St Sixtus off
to his martyrdom. St Lawrence came to the place where they
had taken the saint and approached him, saying: 'Fair father,
what shall I do? I have distributed all the treasures. I have given
them to God's poor. Father, where will you go without me?
When were you ever accustomed to make sacrifice without my
being at your service?'[22] When the men-at-arms heard this, they
came from all sides and seized him, because of the treasures
whose existence he revealed in saying that he had given them to
the poor. They had him guarded by a man-at-arms, and then led
forth St Sixtus to one side down the slope, along with two of his
companions, Felicissimus and Agapitus, whom I mentioned
above.[23] There they beheaded all three. The Christians buried
the bodies and then founded a church there in order to serve

God and pray to him, *to whom is the honour and glory for ever and ever*.[24] (203–42)

After the death of Pope Sixtus, the knights of the Capitoline Hill detained his deacon, St Lawrence, who was the archdeacon and treasurer.[25] The tribune Artimius then came to Decius, saying: 'Lord, your men-at-arms have detained a miscreant, who is responsible for their treasures. I have heard him called Lawrence.' Decius said: 'Go to the provost and tell him to bring him at once.' He left and told him this, and when they heard the order they bound his hands and brought him before Decius. Decius was elated because of the treasures, which he coveted.[26] He asked him repeatedly where they were and St Lawrence made no reply, for he wanted the perfidious tyrant to be driven to anger on this account.[27] Decius heard that he was saying nothing and handed him over to Valerian who, as provost of the city, had great power over everyone.[28] He told him to attempt in due form to make him tell him what he had done with them. (243–70)

Valerian passed him on to Hippolytus, one of his officers who was his deputy and in charge of the gaol, and he took him straight to his dwelling.[29] In the prison St Lawrence found a pagan of high lineage, who had committed some crime or other for which he had been imprisoned. He had been there a long time. Because he was of high birth, the authorities did not want to put him to death, but, not daring to let him go, they kept him imprisoned in cruel conditions. As a result of the suffering he had experienced and the length of time he had been detained, he had wept so much that he could see nothing. His name was Lucillus and he had been blind for a very long time. The holy man St Lawrence said to him that if he were willing to believe in Jesus Christ he would see better than he had ever seen. Lucillus said that he was willing to believe, so St Lawrence baptized him immediately and God restored to him the sight which he had lost earlier.[30] Lucillus said: 'May Jesus Christ be praised, as he should be, because he deigned to visit me and to give light to me through St Lawrence. Formerly I was blind and now I can see. Jesus Christ, I give thanks to you!' (271–302)

The news spread and the blind and the lame came, the feverish and the *paralysed*, and those languishing on account of *dropsy*.[31]

They begged him to have mercy on them, and Jesus Christ in his great mercy gave them all back their health because of his love for them. Let us give thanks to him for this and honour him for his miracles, his signs and the good deeds which he has performed for all Christians. May God and his power be praised. May he permit us to act in such a way that he is so satisfied with us that we may be allowed to come to his glory and to have sovereign joy in that place where one will enjoy delight without suffering.[32] (303–18)

Hippolytus, who was responsible for guarding the prisoners in his dwellings, heard about the marvels and the miracles which had taken place there. He came to the prison and told the saint to tell him where to find the treasures. St Lawrence then told him that if he were willing to believe in Jesus Christ he would show him the treasures and he would have everlasting life. When Hippolytus heard this, he replied at once to St Lawrence: 'If you do as you say and accomplish this, I shall do what you have asked of me.' Oh, Jesus, all-powerful King, how great are your miracles![33] It is no use admonishing a man whom you wish to inspire. If he is in any way disposed towards you, you will soon have transformed him from evil to good. He who turns his heart towards you should have little fear of loss or damage, or of peril, pain or suffering, or of any harm which anyone could do to him. Scripture says indisputably: 'If God is with us, who is against us?'[34] He who has God with him should care little for another's pride or knowledge. For we find it written in another place, where God is speaking to his apostles: 'When you come before kings and counts, or before provosts and viscounts, do not give any thought to what you should say, for the words you should use will be given to you at that time.'[35] (319–53)

You have heard what a fine response was made to St Lawrence by Hippolytus, who was accustomed to torturing people. God had very swiftly given him a change of heart and made him disposed towards him and filled him with his grace. Hearing his reply, St Lawrence prepared the fonts, blessing them and making the sign of the cross over them. Lawrence said: 'Do you believe in Jesus Christ?' '*I believe*', replied Hippolytus.[36] 'And do you believe that he is God the Father and the Son and that he is the Holy Ghost?' '*I believe*,' Hippolytus answered. Then they immersed him three times in the name of the Trinity. They gave him new life in God's name and then along with him St Lawrence baptized his whole household, nineteen in all, who received baptism in God's name because of the teaching of St Lawrence. They were later to suffer great torment on God's behalf, as you will hear further on in the story. To God be the honour and the glory. For all the good things he has done for us, may his precious name be praised![37] (353–80)

Decius then gave orders for St Lawrence to be brought before him. Valerian summoned him, and Hippolytus went to the prison, where he said to him: 'Lawrence, fair friend, Valerian has sent me here. On behalf of Decius I have been ordered to take you before him.' St Lawrence replied: 'Let us both go straight to him at once. Let us not fear him or his household, for great glory is prepared for me and also for you.' They both went along joyfully and made their way to the place where Valerian was holding his session. Then Valerian told the saint to tell him where to find the treasure, and St Lawrence said: 'Allow me a delay of three days and you will see them.' Valerian said: 'Let this be granted to you as you have asked.' He told Decius what he had done, and St Lawrence departed. Throughout the city, where he had distributed the treasures, Lawrence gathered all the poor people he could find (they had already used the treasures for food and drink)[38] and hid them in the house belonging to Hippolytus, his companion. (381–410)

On the third day Decius Caesar was sitting on the emperor's seat, and the nobles of the senate were there.[39] They were holding court and making judgements when Lawrence brought in the poor people whom he had assembled. He said in a loud voice, so that everyone could hear: 'Here is the treasure, which is not missing. It cannot decrease, rather it will increase. It is such that it will not diminish.'[40] Valerian became distraught, and in the presence of Decius he rose and said to St Lawrence in everyone's hearing: 'Come! Abandon your sorcery and sacrifice to our gods or we shall punish you! You will sacrifice to our gods or you will be tortured and killed!' St Lawrence said to the unbeliever: 'Oh, you disciple of the devil, to whom are you saying that a Christian should worship the devil like a pagan? It is not part of doctrine that a Christian should worship any god who is deaf and dumb. For they are made of gold, of silver and brass,[41] and they are deaf, dumb and of no value. Holy Scripture calls them idols, for they are the product of human hands. Now let it be your business to make this judgement: what should everyone worship, something that man makes, or him who has made him?' (411–41)

Decius said: 'What is all this? Who is it who makes, and what is it that man makes?'[42] Lawrence said: 'Your god, which I see here, is what man makes, and it does nothing, for it does neither evil nor good. It is made by human manufacture. According to reason a human creature should not worship something manufactured or dishonour his creator. Indeed, when he worships something which has been made he dishonours himself, for a created being is more noble than a created object. What anyone makes is simply what that person makes, but God does everything, and everything moves through him. It is he who makes, for he made everything in six days of the week, just as we find it written in the psalter that everything was made as soon as he had spoken it.[43] He made known everything which pleased him, and whatever is and has been was created. He who created everything through what he said is he who makes, for he made everything out of nothing.' (442–63)

Decius Caesar replied to him: 'Who is it who made the whole world out of nothing?'

St Lawrence replied: 'God, our father, Jesus Christ, our saviour. He is the creator of the whole world. Heaven, the sea and the round world, hell and the four elements function entirely according to his command. He wants to rid us of the suffering which everyone experienced because of the evil endowment of Adam and his wife Eve. In order to rescue us from the enemy, he was born of the Virgin, contrary to nature but as a sign of his power. Through his power, and not according to nature, the creator made himself a creature. God engendered his son without a mother, the Virgin conceived her son without a father, the Virgin conceived, the Virgin had a child. She was a virgin afterwards and a virgin before.[44] For our redemption our lord endured suffering. Through his passion and his death there was life and comfort for us, since for us his death and passion were redemption from death. That death was not death; it was rather salvation from death to life, because through the passion of Jesus we have comfort and salvation. The first fruit gave us death, and this one on the cross gave us life. Through a tree we were all destroyed and through the wood of a tree we have life and salvation.[45] As that tree bore the fruit by which we were all destroyed, this tree bore the fruit which gave us life. That one bore death in the apple and this one life in human flesh. He who ate that fruit died, but he who eats this one will live in the glory of paradise, where you, Jesus, reign and dwell. On the day of judgement you will return and judge the good and the wicked. Those who have done evil will have evil. They who have done good will have good, in that sovereign kingdom above where Jesus, whom I serve, whom I worship and whom I hold as creator, lives in Trinity.' (464–515)

When Decius Caesar heard what he said, he almost died of anger. He ordered him to be stripped and beaten with wild-rose branches, and the men-at-arms carried out the tyrant's commands. They stripped St Lawrence and beat him, completely naked, with wild-rose branches, so that his entire body become covered in blood.[46] Whilst he was undergoing this torment, he cried out sweetly: 'I give thanks to God, my Lord, who has visited me in this way and enlightened me with his grace, because he wishes to add me to his servants. Jesus, may I praise you. This beating is not torment.' He said to Decius: 'Oh, alas! Unhappy one, you are going mad with anger and I am not the only one who is being tormented!' (516–35)

Decius saw that he would not change his mind, so he ordered him to be brought to his feet again. When he had been raised up, he had brought before him cruel instruments of torture of all kinds, made from wood, from iron, from lead and from stones. Never had any instrument been made which he did not have shown to God's faithful servant.[47] Decius said to St Lawrence: 'Do you not see all these instruments of torture which have been brought out here for you? You will be tortured by each one if you refuse to worship our gods and to abandon your foolish error.' St Lawrence said to the tormentor: 'Renounce your god, worship mine! I do not fear these pains at all. To me they are glory, to you torment. I shall never know such distress on God's behalf that it is not sweet meat to me.'[48] Decius then asked him: 'Since torment is sweet meat to you, where then are the excommunicated ones, the foolish renegade Christians?[49] Tell me where they are, point them out to me! I shall have them come and eat with you the food which you praise so much.' (536–62)

St Lawrence replied to the tyrant: 'Why do you ask after them? They have no desire for your meats, nor do they have any fear of your instruments of torture. Their names are already written down with their lord in paradise above.'[50] Decius had him brought down and taken with him, bound, to the palace of Tiberius, so that there could be a public hearing concerning what he in his faith had done. Decius went to the temple and opened his tribunal there. When he had taken his seat, he sent for St Lawrence. The entire senate was with him and when St Lawrence arrived Decius said to him: 'Abandon your folly, humble yourself before our gods. Do honour and sacrifice to them, or I shall exact punishment on your body. Do not trust your treasures to prevent your body from being treated shamefully. For your treasure will never be great enough to protect you against death. Put an end to the pains of the torments and bring forth the treasures, and tell me where the Christians are who despise our gods. I want to put them to death and make them suffer, and rid the city of them. Abandon your error, give it up, and make sacrifice to our gods! Do not think that what you possess can be of any use against me, or that riches in gold and silver can protect you from my torture. You have a great trust in your treasure when you do not sacrifice to our gods.' St Lawrence replied: 'It is true. I trust in my treasure so much that I have no fear of you. I trust in him in whom I believe, and I have such confidence in my treasure that I do not fear you or what you do. I believe so strongly in the heavenly treasure that I do not fear earthly torment. You will never get hold of it, by any torture whatsoever. I have given it all away to poor people. God will be my guarantor and I take comfort from this. Whatever you are able to do to me, do it now.' (563–613)

When Decius Caesar heard him, he almost died from anger and scorn. Then he had Lawrence beaten, tormented and given great blows with huge sticks. Amidst this torment, St Lawrence said: 'Jesus, lord, I give thanks to you for this joy which I am now experiencing and for that which I shall have afterwards! Cruel tyrant, now you can see that I have complete confidence in my treasure. I am winning a victory over your torments; to me the pain I am feeling is glory. Whatever you do is a delight to me!' Then Decius yelled out, saying: 'You are full of sorcery and that is how you overcome our torments. Now you will have another form of torture.' (614–30)

Then he had the *laminas* brought out, a very horrible form of torture, as the Romans tell us.[51] These were great plates of iron, and the tyrant had them placed burning hot against the saint's sides. Everything the plate touched was burnt and consumed. It burnt his sides and his back, burning his flesh right down to the bone. Lawrence then said: 'Jesus, God, true king, help me, lord, have mercy on me! When I was accused in your name, I did not deny you, rather did I acknowledge you. When they questioned me, I proclaimed you *to be Jesus, the son of God.*[52] You are Jesus and God, the true father, and saviour of the whole world.' Seeing that his torments were of no avail, Decius was very distressed. He had the plates removed and had him raised off the ground, saying to the valiant St Lawrence: 'I see that you have the art of enchantment. But even if you have brought my instruments of torture to nothing, you will not deceive me by your magic arts. By all the gods which I worship, I swear that I shall have you die a painful death, unless you first worship my god and honour him with a sacrifice.' (631–59)

St Lawrence said: 'I fear no torment and I renounce you and your god completely. Whatever you want to do, do it at once. I shall receive it in the name of Jesus.' Decius heard what he said and was very angry. At once they stripped him naked and beat him severely with *plunbatis*. I shall tell you what instrument of torment that was. It was a square-cut club, weighted with nails of molten lead.[53] With this they beat him severely and all his limbs were covered with blood. Over his entire body they made great wounds, deep, horrible and ugly. Then in the midst of his anguish he said: 'Glorious God, lord, receive my spirit.' Then they heard a voice from heaven saying: 'Greater suffering is about to come to you than you have had so far.' Decius heard the voice and said: 'Oh, Roman people, hear how the voice of the devil comforts this unbeliever. He does not fear either our god or me, nor is he afraid of prince or king. He is so full of enchantments that he is not afraid of pain or torments. Take him for me and beat him on my behalf. Torture him with all forms of torture!' (660–89)

Then the Romans threw him down on to a structure called a *catasta*. That was a scaffold where prisoners used to be confined.[54] There they inflicted great torment on him, but the saint said with a smile: 'God and father, in whom I believe, lord, have mercy on me![55] Comfort your servant in your compassion and in such a way that these people know that you are God who can redeem everything and give good comfort to those who in this world will suffer harm, pain and grief for love of you. Be mindful of your servant and display your great power!' As soon as he had said this prayer, a pagan, Romanus by name, sprang forward and fell at his feet, saying to him: 'Have mercy on me! I believe in Jesus Christ, your God, for I saw standing before you a young man in a white tunic, who was wiping away the blood from your wounds. For the love of God, baptize me in the name of Jesus, your creator, who deigned, through his angel, to visit you and to comfort you in this peril and torment.'[56] (690–718)

On hearing this, Decius said to Valerian, who was present: 'We are betrayed and deceived by magic and by enchantment!' Then he ordered his men to untie him from the *catasta* and, when he had been removed, ordered him to be handed over to the custody of Hippolytus but not to be taken away from the palace. Romanus took a little jug and, bringing it full of water to the saint, he begged him to baptize him in the name of Jesus Christ, his lord. St Lawrence received the water, made the sign of the cross over it, and blessed it. Then he baptized him in Jesus' name. (690–734)

When Decius heard this, he had Romanus come before him at once, for he wanted to hear what his faith was. Before Decius had put any questions to him, Romanus cried out and said to the tyrant: 'I am a Christian, thanks be to God.' They took him outside the city, to a gate called Salaria, and there because of his love for God they cut off his head. That day is still celebrated as his feast-day, the fifth calend of August.[57] May God for love of him grant a reward to those who keep this day, or those who honour him in God's name.[58] After he had been beheaded, Justin, a priest who had been ordained by St Sixtus, came for the body at night and with full celebration of the funeral rites they buried him in a crypt. (735–55)[59]

This man died as a good Christian, and that night Decius and Valerian deliberated about how they would treat St Lawrence. They went straight from the temple of Jupiter to the baths of Olympias.[60] In Rome *thermae* are a place where pagans are accustomed to hold games.[61] They passed by the theatre of Augustus, which is beside the palace of Sallust.[62] There Decius had his tribunal set up and he and his knights took their seats. That night he ordered St Lawrence to be brought before him. Hippolytus was full of sorrow and he shed tears of pity and compassion. Lawrence said: 'Do not weep, friend, but keep silent and rejoice, for where I am going I shall have victory. Glory is prepared for me in heaven, up above with the archangels.' (756–69)

Hippolytus replied to the saint: 'I am a Christian and I believe in Jesus. So why am I not going with you? Why am I not going with you to die, for I want to depart to glory?'[63] 'Have patience,' said St Lawrence. 'Keep God concealed here within your heart. But when I send for you, hear my voice and come to me!' (770–85)

Decius, full of anger and evil, sat at his seat on the tribunal. In order to frighten St Lawrence and prevent his glorification he had all his instruments of torture displayed in the sight of his people. The instruments were so hideous and so awful to name that there is no one of human flesh, neither I nor anyone else, who could describe them.[64] When Decius saw the instruments, he said angrily to St Lawrence: 'Lay aside your magic devices and tell me at once about your lineage.' St Lawrence said: 'I am Spanish, but from childhood I have been raised here. I received baptism in my childhood and have placed my trust in Jesus Christ. I learnt grammar and letters, history and other writings, and I have dedicated my youth and my whole life entirely to theology.'[65] Decius replied: 'Truly you are a theologian by enchantment! You know so much about the divine law that you do not fear any god, nor me, nor peril or pain or suffering, nor any torment which I can inflict upon you.' (786–813)

St Lawrence replied to the tyrant: 'I believe so strongly in God my Father that I have no fear of any action opposed to my belief.' This distressed Decius greatly and he had him beaten in the teeth with stones, saying: 'An evil night has come; it will be spent entirely on you, in pain, hurt and tortures.' Then St Lawrence replied to him: 'In my night there is no darkness, for everything is shining brightly.'[66] The evil infidels struck him again in the mouth. St Lawrence remained cheerful, saying: 'God be praised! Jesus Christ, I give thanks to you, for you are Almighty God.'[67] Then Decius said: 'Bring forward a bed of iron and let Lawrence, the bold and the arrogant, be placed on it.' A bed was brought before him, made like an iron grill with three bars across it.[68] They set it down in front of Decius and placed St Lawrence on it, naked. Then the men-at-arms brought in burning coals in pans and spread them beneath the gridiron, roasting and grilling St Lawrence. In a frenzy Decius told the saint to make sacrifice to his gods. St Lawrence said to the wretch: 'I have offered myself as a sacrifice to God, to whom I am given, for an afflicted spirit acts as a sacrifice to the Creator.' I understand this on the authority of the prophet David, who said: ' "God does not despise an afflicted spirit." '[69] (814–53)

St Lawrence lay on the gridiron and they made him suffer over his whole body. The men-at-arms blew on the coals and spread them beneath the valiant man. They pressed him down against the gridiron with the iron forks they held in their hands. St Lawrence said to Decius: 'Now you can see, unhappy wretch, that your coals are a comfort to me and a torment and misery to you. God well knows that when I was accused I did not deny him; I recognized him as God, and when questioned I proclaimed him. Now I am being burnt, I give thanks to him for it!'[70] (854–67)

On the gridiron where he lay he gave thanks to Jesus Christ. He turned his thoughts towards this verse: 'We passed through water and fire, you led us to comfort, we give you *thanks*.'[71] Valerian, who was provost, said to the saint: 'Where are the fires which you promised to our gods when you said that you would burn them?' St Lawrence replied to him, saying to the princes who were there: 'Oh, unfortunate and unhappy ones, you who are beside yourselves with madness! Have you not realized that I am not being burnt by this fire? Nor do I feel it on my flesh or my bones; rather it is comfort and repose for me.' All those present felt horror and compassion at Decius' cruelty in having him roasted alive in that way. Then St Lawrence said with a smile, his face composed and his appearance fair: 'God, may I praise you for having deigned to comfort me here.'[72] He opened his eyes and then said to Decius whom he saw before him: 'Unhappy one, turn me the other way. Eat on this side, it is very well cooked!'[73] He gave glory and thanks to God, saying: '*Father* omnipotent, Jesus Christ, I give thanks to you who have given me this wisdom to have merit in your eyes so that I shall enter your gates.'[74] So saying, the saint gave up his spirit to God. The soul of the saint went straight to heaven. His body remained on the gridiron. (868–907)

When Decius had done this, he departed with the provost. They went to the palace of Tiberius, leaving behind St Lawrence's body. Before daybreak, Hippolytus took it away with great tenderness. He closed the eyes, joined the feet together and anointed him all over with balm. He wrapped him in a shroud and then summoned Justin the priest to him, now that Decius had departed, leaving the body on the gridiron over the coals. Justin came to the noble man, sad, grief-stricken and in tears. They took away St Lawrence's body and carried it *to the Tiburtine Gate*, where they kept watch over it until nightfall.[75] They buried it in a crypt which they found at the Tiburtine Gate, *in the Field of Verano*, the meadow which belonged *to a certain widow* to whom St Lawrence had earlier given health and salvation.[76] There they buried him in due form on the fourth of the ides of *August*, and they fasted for three days, with vigils and mortifications.[77] All the Christians wept and grieved. Justin sang Mass and gave *communion* to everyone, in honour of God and in his memory.[78] Let us pray to him that he will give us glory, in that place where he reigns in permanent joy, and let us suffer no peril or pain, or lose sovereign joy because of any act of which we might be guilty. Rather may he allow us, oh Jesus, to act in such a way that we can have comfort and the glory of paradise, in that place where you reign and live. Amen. (908–49)

COMMENTARY

St Catherine

References to the Anglo-Norman text of the *Life of St Catherine* are by line number to the edition by William MacBain, *The Life of St. Catherine by Clemence of Barking*, ANTS 18 (Oxford: Blackwell for ANTS, 1964). References to the Latin source of the *Life of St. Catherine* are by page and line number to the edition by E. J. Dobson and S. R. T. O. d'Ardenne, *Seinte Katerine*, EETS, ss 7 (Oxford: Oxford University Press for the EETS 1981), pp. 132–203. We are indebted to these editions, to the investigation of literary and devotional contexts by Catherine Batt, 'Clemence of Barking's Transformations of *courtoisie* in *La vie de sainte Catherine d'Alexandrie*', in *Translation in the Middle Ages*, ed. Roger Ellis (*New Comparisons*, 12 (1991), pp. 102–23), and to the helpful commentary and notes in the translation of the early Middle English *Katerine* by Anne Savage and Nicholas Watson, *Anchoritic Spirituality: Ancrene Wisse and Associated Works* (Mahwah, NJ: Paulist Press, 1991), pp. 422–8.

[1] **1–50:** Clemence's Latin source, the long version of the so-called 'Vulgate' passion (see Introduction, pp. xxvii–xxviii), often included in its medieval manuscripts a prologue on the value of writing saints' lives and on the example of constancy offered by Catherine as a member of the weaker sex (*Vulgate*, pp. 144/1–45/32). Clemence ignores the *Vulgate* prologue, if indeed it was in her text of the source, and writes a prologue using topics commonly found in the prologues to Anglo-Norman hagiographic and devotional works. On these, see Karl Uitti, 'The Clerkly Narrator Figure in Old French Hagiography and Romance', *Medioevo Romanzo*, 2 (1975), 394–408; Paul Jones, *Prologue and Epilogue in Old French Saints' Lives before 1400* (Philadelphia, Pa: University of Pennsylvania Press, 1933); and J. Wogan-Browne, 'Wreaths of Thyme: the Female Translator in Anglo-Norman Hagiography', in *The Medieval Translator 4*, ed. Roger Ellis and Ruth

Evans (Exeter: University of Exeter Press, 1994), pp. 46–65. With vv.
1–6 of *St Catherine* compare Marie de France's prologue to her *Lais*,
ed. A. Ewert (Oxford: Blackwell, 1944), p. 3, vv. 1–8, and her *Fables*,
ed. A. Ewert and R. C. Johnston (Oxford: Blackwell, 1942), p. 1, vv.
1–10. Clemence's metaphor of 'fruit' (v. 3), where Marie has the more
usual 'flower' (*Lais*, v. 8), preludes the theme of Christ as the fruit of
the cross (see vv. 965–1000).

[2] 7–14: where Marie de France's authorities for the nature and value
of literary transmission are classical (Priscian and 'the philosophers',
Lais, Prologue, vv. 10, 17), as is the source of exemplary material ('the
philosophers', *Fables*, Prologue, v. 5), the figure of Christ fulfils all
these functions in Clemence's prologue. On Christ's maternal role of
nourishing and feeding (vv. 13–14), see Caroline Walker Bynum, *Jesus
as Mother: Studies in the Spirituality of the High Middle Ages* (Berkeley,
Los Angeles and London: University of California Press, 1982), esp.
ch. iv.

[3] 35: the text referred to is thought by some scholars to be a dramatized
version of the *Life of St Catherine*, part of which is extant in
Manchester, John Rylands University Library, MS French 6. See E. C.
Fawtier-Jones, 'Les Vies de Sainte Catherine d'Alexandrie en ancien
français', *Romania*, 56 (1930), 80–104 (pp. 100–3). It is of course also
possible that Clemence is referring here to some other vernacular
version of which we have no extant traces. MacBain (vv. 1849–50,
1861, 2359, 2639, 2641nn.) indicates lines from the fragment which
are closely paralleled in *Catherine*.

[4] 37–46: Anglo-Norman prologue topics include many variations on
contempt of the world and the transience of nobility, wealth and
worldly achievement. See A. R. Harden, 'The "Ubi sunt" Theme in
Three Anglo-Norman Saints' Lives', *Romance Notes*, 1 (1959), 53–5;
and Jones, *Prologue and Epilogue*. Cf. *Lawrence*, vv. 22–6.

[5] 56: the empress Helena (*c.* AD 250–330) was the discoverer of the
true cross as well as the mother of Constantine, the emperor who
established Christianity as a state religion. She is not mentioned in the
Latin source. Helena had a particular cult in England and was
sometimes said to be of British origin. See Farmer, *s.n.* 'Helen'.

[6] 61: at least two figures from the early fourth century seem to be

conflated in the legend's account of Catherine's persecutor. M. Aurelius Valerius Maxentius shared the Western empire with Constantine for a time and was emperor in Rome from AD 306 to 312, when he was defeated by Constantine. It was before their battle that Constantine, according to Eusebius, was converted by his famous vision of the cross: see A. H. M. Jones, *Constantine and the Conversion of Europe*, rev. edn (Harmondsworth: Penguin Books, 1972), pp. 98–100. Galerius Valerius Maximinus, originally called Daza, persecuted Christians in the East and published an edict in AD 306 demanding temple sacrifices (see *Catherine*, vv. 96–104). He carried out further persecutions in AD 311–12 and died after being defeated by Licinius in AD 313: see W. Smith, *Dictionary of Greek and Roman Biography and Mythology*, II (London: John Murray, 1854), p. 985. The identity of the persecutors is frequently transposed or composite in saints' lives (for a further example, see note to *Lawrence*, v. 95).

[7] 70–4: these lines are without equivalent in the *Vulgate*. For analogous proverbial expressions, see Elisabeth Schulze-Busacker, *Proverbes et expressions proverbiales dans la littérature narrative du moyen-âge français: Recueil et analyse* (Geneva and Paris: Slatkine, 1985), no. 1092, pp. 235–6, 'Le mal ne se peut celer'.

[8] 91: Anglo-Norman *pretoire* for the Latin source's *pretorium regis* (*Vulgate*, 146/54) is not listed in *AND*, but compare AN *pretour* (Med. Lat. *pretor*, 'reeve, provost') and classical Latin *praetorium*, 'the commander's quarters, official residence of the governor of a province, palace'. The word is used of Pilate's quarters in accounts of Christ's passion (for Anglo-Norman and Old French examples, see Tobler-Lommatzsch, *s.v.* 'pretoire').

[9] 95: Anglo-Norman *devant le pretoire* for Latin *sedens pro tribunali* (*Vulgate*, 146/54–5).

[10] 97–118: Clemence puts the emperor's commands into direct speech uttered by the provost (vv. 97–104) and adds a passage of commentary on the motives and responses of Maxentius' subjects, using the same kind of proverbial register as for the earlier comment on the emperor (see note to vv. 70–4).

[11] 135–6: on Catherine's youth and its courtly connotations, see Batt,

p. 112 and n. 53. See also vv. 1507–9, 1976–9, 2529–30; *Lawrence*, note to vv. 890–3.

[12] 141–4: such a formal education in *disputatio* would be exceptional among contemporary Anglo-Norman nobles for any except professional clerics and scholars and was never institutionally offered to medieval women. The word *dialecticien* (v. 143) is relatively rare in Anglo-Norman, though not unparalleled. It is not present in the Latin source, which suggests that Clemence was aware of the curriculum of the 'liberal arts' (*Vulgate*, 148/85). For an account of the literacy of some post-Conquest holy women, see Bella Millett, 'Women in No Man's Land: English Recluses and the Development of Vernacular Literature in the Twelfth and Thirteenth Centuries', in *Women and Literature in Britain, 1150–1500*, ed. Carol M. Meale (Cambridge: Cambridge University Press, 1993), pp. 86–103. See also M. T. Clanchy, *From Memory to Written Record: England 1066–1307*, 2nd edn (Oxford: Blackwell, 1993), pp. 189–96, 252.

[13] 145–58: there is no equivalent in the Latin source for this passage. Clemence invokes key oppositions in the rhetoric of courtly love (pain in joy, and joy in suffering, vv. 153–4), whilst showing how Catherine's chaste love transcends them. Batt (n. 54) compares this 'chaste and pure' love with that defined in a medieval French version of the Song of Songs. See further MacBain, 'Some Religious and Secular Uses of the Vocabulary of *fin'amor* in the Early Decades of the Northern French Narrative Poem', *French Forum*, 13 (1988), 260–76.

[14] 159–64: under Anglo-Norman law, orphan noblewomen could inherit, but were frequently under pressure to remarry, or, if they did not enter a religious house, to pay a fine for the privilege of not marrying. See Cecily Clark, 'After 1066: The Factual Evidence', in Christine Fell, Cecily Clark and Elizabeth Williams, *Women in Anglo-Saxon England* (London: British Museum Publications, 1984), pp. 149–50; and Sue Sheridan Walker, 'The Marrying of Feudal Wards in Medieval England', *Studies in Medieval Culture*, 4 (1974), 209–24. The Latin source and the early Middle English life explain (*Vulgate*, 147/75–148/77; *Katerine*, 6/30–4) that Katherine maintained her household (rather than entering a life of religion) not because she wanted a great retinue or to be a great lady, but to carry out her ancestral responsibility to the estate's dependants. Disposing of wealth

which was surplus to that required for maintenance, as Catherine does (v. 163), is both conventional for saints (Lucy and Cecilia are two other prominent examples) and a reflection of the actual practice of Anglo-Norman noblewomen who entered the religious life.

¹⁵ 189: the Latin source for the first time calls Catherine *beata virgo*, 'blessed virgin' (*Vulgate*, 149/105; previously *puella*, 147/71, AN *pulcele*, v. 135). Clemence, in accordance with a major theme of the Life introduced in v. 31 and developed in the expansion at vv. 145–58, translates as 'God's beloved' (AN *l'amie Deu*, with *amie* in the sense of both 'beloved' and 'lover').

¹⁶ 209–16: contrast between God's living creation and pagan inanimate idols is a commonplace of saints' arguments against pagan tyrants. See also vv. 1302–8; and cf. Psalms 114 (115): 3–8. It is a pervasive theme in *Lawrence* (see esp. vv. 430–63, note to vv. 443–515 and pp. 100–101 below). See 'Saints and Simulacra', in Michael Camille, *The Gothic Idol: Ideology and Image-Making in Medieval Art* (Cambridge: Cambridge University Press, 1989), pp. 115–28.

¹⁷ 283–92: Catherine's application of her argument to Maxentius' own lordship is without equivalent at this point in the *Vulgate* but transposes a passage from the saint's previous speech (*Vulgate*, 151/136–41).

¹⁸ 317–20: vv. 318 and 320 are a scribal intervention in MS A and do not occur in MSS WP. They are not translated here. Professor MacBain confirms (private communication) that they will be omitted from his forthcoming re-edition of the text.

¹⁹ 327–8: these lines have no equivalent in the *Vulgate* and they perhaps reflect Clemence's awareness of the formal art of letter-writing (*ars dictaminis*). Letter-writing is a genre used relatively frequently by medieval noblewomen. See the introduction to *Dear Sister: Medieval Women and the Epistolary Genre in the Middle Ages*, ed. Karen Cherewaytuk and Ulrike Wiethaus (Philadelphia, Pa: University of Pennsylvania Press, 1993), pp. 1–19.

²⁰ 331–2: *rethorien* (v. 331) is a relatively rare term in the vernacular. Clemence seems here to have provided a gloss for it in v. 332.

²¹ 335: the emperor's term for Catherine (*plaideresse*, 'advocate, pleader', v. 335) is rare and is perhaps a nonce creation feminizing the

term (AN *plaidur*, *-er*, *-our*, 'advocate, pleader'). The Latin source's *contionatrix* (*Vulgate*, 154/215) is a feminized medieval form of classical Latin *contionator*, 'demagogue, agitator'. In its twelfth-century masculine form it is used to mean 'public speaker, preacher', or 'suitor at a county court'. In the rarer feminine form it appears either to have been figurative or to have meant 'speaker'. See R. E. Latham, *A Dictionary of Medieval Latin from British Sources* (London: Oxford University Press for the British Academy, 1981), *s.v.* 'contionatrix'.

22 352–6: these two sentences concerning Catherine's effect on the spectators and the emperor have no equivalent in the Latin source.

23 385–93: in the *Vulgate* at this point (*Vulgate*, 156/238–9) the saint quotes I Corinthians 1:19 (itself a quotation of Isaiah 29:4) and Psalms 114 (115):3–8 on God's destruction of worldly wisdom and idols. Clemence's St Catherine explains instead how she fell in love with the Trinitarian God once she understood his gospel.

24 455–74: this commentary on the leading pagan clerk is an addition without equivalent in the *Vulgate*. Like many of Clemence's expansions, it has a proverbial character and many analogies, if not any specific known source, in medieval sermons and penitential material. For comparable material in later medieval French, see James W. Hassell, *Middle French Proverbs, Sentences and Proverbial Phrases*, Subsidia Medievalia 12 (Toronto: Pontifical Institute of Mediaeval Studies, 1982), *s.v.* 'envie' (E54–E57, pp. 103–4); *orgueil* (O82–O88, p. 186).

25 508–22: these lines on Catherine's comfort in her good intention (AN *bone entente*, v. 508; *bon vuleir*, vv. 510 (MS W), 511, 514, 521) are without equivalent in the *Vulgate*. The saint's condition contrasts with Maxentius in his soliloquies as he bemoans his conflicted will (*voleir*, *vuleir*, see vv. 2204–16, 2418–20) and provides a model for the audience's *bon voleir* (v. 2648).

26 524: it is unclear whether AN *chevalerie* in v. 524 (*force a sa chevalerie*, all manuscripts) should be taken as referring to God's chivalric qualities or his heavenly militia. The former is supported by the life's emphasis on God as Catherine's lover, the latter by the life's inclusion of several angelic interventions. The Latin source suggests that the possessive refers to Catherine: *imperterrita militie sue agonem Domino commendabat* (*Vulgate*, 159/295–6), 'undisturbed by her

[war] service she entrusted the contest [*agonem*] to the Lord' (taking *militie sue* as ablative). MacBain glosses *chevalerie* as 'chivalric encounter, combat', presumably taking *sa* as referring to Catherine. The line would then translate 'and strength in her fight'.

²⁷ 539–44: see Matthew 10:18–19; Mark 13:9–11; Luke 21:12–15 (*Vulgate*, 159/299–302).

²⁸ 581–2: the ultimate source of this motif is Revelation 14:3–4, where the 144,000 who sing a new song are male virgins. In its feminized form and combined with the image of virgins (rather than the Holy Jerusalem itself, Revelation 21:2) as brides of the Lamb, the choir of virgins is a commonplace of both patristic and medieval writing (see also vv. 1779–81 below; and see further Santha Bhattacharji, '*Pearl* and the Liturgical "Common of Virgins"', *Medium Ævum*, 64 (1995), 37–50 (pp. 44–5). In the *Vulgate* (160/319–20) the angel concludes the speech by naming himself as Michael, but Clemence omits (or possibly did not have in her source text) this identification.

²⁹ 585–6: this sentence is an addition by Clemence. In the *Vulgate* the action passes directly from the saint's response to the angel, to Maxentius on his pretorium seat in the morning (*Vulgate*, 160/321–3). Such small details are important in creating the distinctive spatial sense of the Anglo-Norman narrative and in allowing us to move outside the perspectives of the protagonists.

³⁰ 595–626: these lines are Clemence's addition. The *Vulgate* mentions the arrival of a crowd of spectators (*Vulgate*, 161/326–7) but does not discuss their perception of the saint. The relation between outward beauty and inward goodness, which is a major theme of the expansion, was of spiritual as well as courtly significance in saints. Their external composure and body language were a further dimension in which grace could be manifested. See the discussion by Walter Simons, 'Reading a Saint's Body: Rapture and Bodily Movement in the *vitae* of Thirteenth-Century Beguines', in *Framing Medieval Bodies*, ed. Sarah Kay and Miri Rubin (Manchester and New York: Manchester University Press, 1994), pp. 10–23 (pp. 14–15). As elsewhere, Clemence expands on the source here by composing the kind of aphoristic moral reflection highly valued in the Middle Ages (cf. Schulze-Busacker, *Proverbes*, pp. 217–23, esp. no. 780, 'Fous est qui se oublie'). *Catherine*, vv. 599–610, is quoted in a fourteenth-century trilingual preaching miscellany

(Cambridge, Trinity College, MS B.14.39, fol. 80ᵛ), under the title 'Proverbia Marie Magdalene', which suggests that they could be unfixed from their original context and read as generally authoritative proverbial truths. (Mary Magdalen was known as the 'apostle of the apostles' because she brought them the news of Christ's resurrection. Together with Catherine herself she is one of the few female figures represented as legitimately preaching in public in the Middle Ages.)

³¹ **678**: in the Latin source Catherine's opponent is said to be the oldest and most experienced, rather than the vainest, of the philosophers (*Vulgate*, 162/349–50).

³² **686–94**: Clemence abbreviates the saint's denunciation of pagan learning. The *Vulgate* at this point offers a magnificently rhetorical denunciation of Homer, Aristotle, Aesculapius, Galen, Philistion and Plato (*Vulgate*, 162/355–163/359).

³³ **703–4**: the *Vulgate* presents the Fall as humanity's exclusion from the delights of paradise through the devil (*Vulgate*, 163/368–9). Clemence adds an account of the deception of Eve through the apple, preluding the thematic significance this fruit will have in Catherine's exposition of Christ as the fruit of the cross (see vv. 965–1000). See also Batt, p. 119 n. 36. For v. 705 we have adopted the reading of MSS WP, 'Ele en duna a sun segnur'; MS A reads 'Ele en mangad e sun segnur' ('She ate some of it and so did her husband').

³⁴ **724–26**: these lines expand the *Vulgate*'s mention of the Virgin (163/370). The painless birth of Christ is traditionally one of the Five Joys of the Virgin Mary, answering the painful childbirth which was Eve's lot after the Fall. For another Marian expansion see vv. 1745–68.

³⁵ **771–80**: these lines are without equivalent in the *Vulgate*, where the saint concludes her speech with the assertion of God's all-embracing power (*Vulgate*, 165/394–5).

³⁶ **781–4**: these lines expand the *Vulgate*, where the clerk simply replies to the saint (*Vulgate*, 165/396). Clemence's clerks are still more threatened and Catherine more directly challenging than in the Latin source.

³⁷ **785–804**: the relation of human and divine in Christ is a much-discussed topic of Christian theology. See *ODCC, s.v.* 'Christology'

(esp. pp. 278–9), 'Incarnation' (esp. pp. 684–5). Throughout the saint's debate with the pagan philosophers, Clemence seems influenced in her expansions on the Latin source by Anselm's *Meditation on Human Redemption* (*S. Anselmi opera omnia*, ed. F. S. Schmitt, vol. III (Edinburgh: Nelson, 1946), pp. 84–91; trans. Benedicta Ward, *The Prayers and Meditations of St Anselm* (Harmondsworth: Penguin Books, 1973), pp. 230–7).

³⁸ 821–2: this sentence is not in the *Vulgate*. The equivalent English expression is used in the early Middle English life of the saint's reading of scripture, 'eauer ha hefde on hali writ ehnen oðer heorte, oftest ba togederes' ('always she had her eyes or her heart on holy scripture, most often both together', *Katerine*, 8/40).

³⁹ 849–50: the meaning of the text is obscure at this point (see MacBain, vv. 849–50n). We have based the translation on the reading in MS W, where the rhymes of this couplet are reversed (see MacBain, p. 27, vv. 849–50, *app. crit.*).

⁴⁰ 895–8: patristic and medieval theologians believed Plato to have anticipated important aspects of Christian theory. This prophecy probably goes back ultimately to *Timaeus* 34A–B, where the world is said to have been 'devised by the ever-existent god for the god who was one day to be' (*Timaeus*, trans. John Warrington (London: Dent, 1965), p. 25). Twelfth-century theological commentary and literary exegesis concerned themselves with the linguistic and theological status of Plato's 'prophecies'. Like the Sibyls (see note to vv. 903–6) classical philosophers could also appear in semi-liturgical prophet plays (*ordo prophetarum*) and in fabricated 'symposia', such as the *Book of the Twenty-Four Philosophers* (cited by Peter Dronke in his *Hermes and the Sibyls: Continuations and Creations* (Cambridge: Cambridge University Press, 1990), esp. pp. 23–5). Since Constantine (*Catherine*, v. 57; *Vulgate*, 145/33) was especially associated with what was understood in the Middle Ages as the Sibyl's prophecy of Christ in Virgil's Fourth Eclogue, it may not be coincidental that the medieval traditions of Plato and the Sibyl are linked in the *Vulgate* life of Catherine.

⁴¹ 901–2: it is not certain whether Anglo-Norman *runt* in v. 901 should be taken to mean a 'clear' or a 'round' sign (see MacBain, v.901n.). The orb held by Christ in medieval representations frequently takes the form of a cross within a circle (see Heather Child and Dorothy Colles,

Christian Symbols Ancient and Modern (London: Bell, 1971), pp. 21, 27–30; E. Kirschbaum *et al.*, *Lexicon der christlichen Ikonographie* (Rome, Freiburg, Basel and Vienna: Herder, 1968–76), vol II col. 569, pl. 4. The 'sign' may perhaps initially have referred to the round world revolving in a circle said in the *Timaeus* to be created in Plato's 'prophecy' of Christ (see *Timaeus*, 34A–B, cited in note to vv. 895–8; and see Dronke, *Hermes and Sibyls*, p. 24).

[42] 903–6: on the Sibylline prophecies in medieval culture, see Bernard McGinn, '*Teste David cum Sibylla*: The Significance of the Sibylline Tradition in the Middle Ages', in *Women of the Medieval World: Essays in Honor of John H. Mundy*, ed. Suzanne F. Wemple and Julius Kirshner (Oxford: Blackwell, 1985), pp. 7–35. For an Anglo-Norman version of the prophecies of the Tiburtine Sybil, see *Le Livre de Sibile by Philippe de Thaon*, ed. Hugh Shields, ANTS 37 (London: ANTS, 1979).

[43] 915–16: this repetition of the Sibyl's saying (cf. vv. 905–6) is not in the Latin source's analysis of the Sibyl and Plato's words (*Vulgate*, 168/457–61). Clemence omits the latter part of the *Vulgate*'s speech and with it the saint's exultation in conquering the philosophers with their own weapons (*Vulgate*, 169/474–6).

[44] 942–1010: Clemence here greatly expands the Latin source, which provides only the skeleton of the argument for this climactic speech (*Vulgate*, 169/485–170/502).

[45] 961–4: these lines have no equivalent in the *Vulgate*. They are very close to Anselm, *Meditation* (trans. Ward, p. 233; cf. *S. Anselmi opera omnia*, ed. F. S. Schmitt, vol. III, p. 87/102–3).

[46] 965–1000: Clemence here further develops the theme of the apple as the fruit of the cross (see note to vv. 703–4). There is a comparable elaboration in *Lawrence*, vv. 494–507. Clemence's Latin source here refers only to the wood of the cross and the tree (*Vulgate*, 169/490–5), an antithesis, as Batt points out (p. 119 n. 35), long established in the liturgy. See, for example, the Preface for the Feast of the Invention quoted in Barbara C. Raw, *Anglo-Saxon Crucifixion Iconography and the Art of the Monastic Revival* (Cambridge: Cambridge University Press, 1990), I. p. 176. On medieval developments of cross motifs and legends, see Evelyn Greenhill, 'The Child in the Tree: A Study of the

Cosmological Tree in Christian Tradition', *Traditio*, 10 (1954), 323–71. Honorius of Autun's influential commentary on the Psalms explicates the fruit of the tree as Christ hanging on it (*PL* 172.276–8), and for a writer of Clemence's Latinity would have been a possible source. The cross as the tree of life is a motif of Anglo-Norman bestiaries, where it is given Christian explication. See *Le Bestiaire de Philippe de Thaün*, ed. Emmanuel Walberg (Lund and Paris: H. Welther, 1900), pp. 90–2, esp. vv. 2519–22; and Guillaume le Clerc, *Le Bestiaire*, ed. Robert Reinsch (Leipzig: Reisland, 1892), pp. 355–6, vv. 3027–53 (this passage is particularly close to the formulations in *Catherine*). The cross and its burden are also the subject of many Anglo-Norman and Middle English devotional lyrics, some of them especially associated with women. For examples, see *The Anglo-Norman Lyric*, ed. David L. Jeffrey and Brian J. Levy, Studies and Texts 93 (Toronto: Pontifical Institute of Mediaeval Studies, 1990), nos 10, 11, 13 and 14; and *English Lyrics of the Thirteenth Century*, ed. Carleton Brown (Oxford: Clarendon Press, 1932; repr. 1971), nos 1, 4, 15, 34–7, 47, 49, 64. For a good example of the adoration of the cross as part of the liturgical experience of Anglo-Norman religious women, see the version of the Office of Our Lady and associated devotions written for early thirteenth-century anchoresses in *Ancrene Riwle: Introduction and Part One*, ed. Robert W. Ackerman and Roger Dahood, Medieval and Renaissance Texts and Studies 31 (Binghamton, NY: MRTS, 1984), pp. 56–7, 68–9. Venantius Fortunatus' beautiful sixth-century hymns on the cross (especially *Vexilla regis prodeunt* and *Pange lingua*) also remained widely influential in the Middle Ages and contain parallels for the motifs used by Clemence. See F. J. E. Raby, *A History of Christian Latin Poetry from the Beginnings to the Close of the Middle Ages*, 2nd edn (Oxford: Clarendon Press, 1953), pp. 88–91. In the fourteenth century, Kathryn de Sutton, abbess of Barking 1363–76, arranged a special extra-liturgical Easter play with a deposition from the cross and an elevation to follow Matins on Easter Day (see Karl Young, *The Drama of the Medieval Church* (Oxford: Clarendon Press, 1933; repr. 1962), vol. I, pp. 166–7. For an analysis of some of the word-play and other features of this rhetorical climax to the debate in *Catherine*, see p. xlvii above.

[47] 1001–10: in the Latin source (*Vulgate*, 169/495–170/502) this passage, as Savage and Watson point out (*Anchoritic Spirituality*,

p. 426 n. 26), is reminiscent of Anselm, *Meditation* (*Opera omnia*, ed. Schmitt, vol. III, 86/59–66; trans. Ward, p. 232), as it is in *Catherine* and in the early Middle English *Katerine*. The thirteenth-century English text, however, elaborates the Latin source with a theologically dated stress on God's deception of the devil (denied by Anselm). Clemence maintains a more Anselmian stress on the redemption of humanity in Christ's humanity: see esp. vv. 1001–5.

[48] 1031–2: for other occurrences of this saying in narrative verse, see Batt, p. 106 and n. 21. See also *Lawrence*, vv. 5–12.

[49] 1011–56: these lines are without equivalent in the *Vulgate*, where the focus is restricted to the philosophers' astonishment and confusion (*Vulgate*, 170/503–6). Clemence's crowd consists of all the auditors of the debate, presumably the populace of Alexandria (see vv. 623–4), as well as Maxentius and his clerks, and we are encouraged to hear the varying voices of the more peopled world of her narrative, as well as the narrative's own commentary on the fickleness of worldly motivations. The varying response of the members of the crowd, not all of whom are immediately converted, is unusual in saints' lives. This passage can thus be seen as part of Clemence's pervasive strategy of making the pagans credible and intelligible, rather than merely sensationalized villains; see p. xxx above.

[50] 1059: we have adopted the reading of MS W (*vus* for MS A's *nus*). See MacBain, note to vv. 1059–70.

[51] 1078–84: Clemence alters the source in order to focus on Catherine's authority. In the *Vulgate*, the leading rhetor alludes to the philosophers' hitherto undefeated supremacy witnessed by all the orators of the East rather than to their mothers (*Vulgate*, 171/516–20). He also says that nothing human speaks in Catherine, but, rather, a divine spirit (*Vulgate*, 171/521–2).

[52] 1140–6: Christian doctrine teaches the necessity of baptism before entering the kingdom of God. Augustine allowed the baptism of blood (i.e. martyrdom) or of desire to be on occasion equivalent to the sacrament of baptism. In adults, baptism is believed to forgive sin and remit its penalties. The philosophers are thus properly anxious as good Christians to be baptized, but can also be properly reassured by the

saint that they need have no concern about their baptism. See *ODCC*, *s.v.*, 'baptism'.

[53] **1154–8:** these two sentences of comment on God's care for his followers have no equivalent in the *Vulgate*.

[54] **1159–70:** this address to the audience is without equivalent in the *Vulgate* and is presumably Clemence's addition. The term 'lords' (AN *segnurs*, v. 1159) suggests an audience of male religious or of mixed lay and religious (i.e. audiences outside as well as within Barking). Although the term's occurrence in manuscript texts copied for nuns suggests that it can be used inclusively, it would hardly be used by a nun writing exclusively for an audience of other nuns. See also the saint's address to the crowd in vv. 1981ff. On the overlap between religious and secular forms of etiquette, see Jonathan Nicholls, *The Matter of Courtesy: Medieval Courtesy Books and the Gawain-Poet* (Cambridge: D. S. Brewer, 1985), ch. 2, 'Courtesy and the Religious Orders'.

[55] **1183–1238:** these lines represent a lengthy expansion of the Latin source. They partly recapitulate and develop themes from the prologue. God feeds and loves us and is the only source of goodness (vv. 1185–1202; cf. vv. 7–14). Although all things are created in goodness, they are prone to change and decay, and God provides both an initial and a continuing source of goodness (vv. 1203–16; cf. vv. 8–10, 16–20). God's goodness is particularly shown in the intactness of the clerks' bodies (vv. 1183–92, 1229–34; see also vv. 1154–8). For medieval anxieties about bodily wholeness, see Caroline Walker Bynum, 'Material Continuity, Personal Survival and the Resurrection of the Body: A Scholastic Discussion in its Medieval and Modern Contexts', in her *Fragmentation and Redemption: Essays on Gender and the Human Body in Medieval Religion* (New York: Zone Books, 1992), pp. 239–97.

[56] **1227:** in this line the form *estuet* is present tense, but MacBain states that 'a preterite would seem to be required by the sense' (p. 89). MS P has a preterite *covint*, and, adopting this reading, one could translate: 'Through death it was fitting that they sought life.'

[57] **1264:** we have followed MacBain, note to v. 1264, in choosing to translate AN *piue* by 'patience'.

[58] 1271–4: these lines translate the Latin source closely (*Vulgate*, 174/577–8), but add an extra stipulation in the mention of dower in v. 1271. (AN *duaire, dower, doaire*, etc.) was the gift of bridegroom to bride and, unlike the dowry brought to the husband by the bride, was (at least in theory) property over which Anglo-Norman wives retained control at their husband's death. See Janet Senderowitz Loengard, '"Of the Gift of Her Husband": English Dower and its Consequences in the Year 1200', in *Women of the Medieval World*, ed. Kirshner and Wemple, pp. 215–55; and Michael M. Sheehan, 'The Influence of Canon Law on the Property Rights of Married Women in England', *Mediaeval Studies*, 25 (1963), 109–24.

[59] 1371–84: these comments on Catherine's motives and Maxentius' wickedness have no equivalent in the *Vulgate*.

[60] 1468–70: in the *Vulgate* the content of these lines is reported as indirect speech (*Vulgate*, 178/659–60).

[61] 1505–6: this sentence has no equivalent in the *Vulgate*. While conceivably due to a different source or manuscript variant, it is also in keeping with the prominence earlier accorded the bodily intactness of the martyred clerks (vv. 1183–1238, esp. vv. 1229–34; and see note to vv. 1183–1238).

[62] 1625–30: the *Vulgate*'s account of the heavenly chorus of virgins who follow the Lamb of God (183/751–2) either was not present in Clemence's source-text or has been omitted in favour of the personal relationship envisaged in vv. 1626–9. The chorus of virgins *is* present in vv. 581–2, 1779–81 and 1847–8.

[63] 1666–96: for homiletic parallels in Anglo-Norman for the motif of transience (here expanded from *Vulgate*, 184/767–75), see Batt, p. 106 nn. 19 and 20. See also note to vv. 37–46 above.

[64] 1720: we follow MacBain (note to v. 1720) in translating 'or' in preference to the manuscript reading *de* ('of').

[65] 1711–34: Clemence makes the Latin source's list of negative qualities (hostility, privation, vexation: *Vulgate*, 184/785–6) more detailed and less abstract (vv. 1713–20; cf. Revelation 21:4). Heaven's perennial bliss, joy and delight (*Vulgate*, 184/787) is retained as 'joy' (vv. 1724–30) and elaborated with a list of the qualities of spiritual

courtliness (AN *charité, honur, plenté, largesce, valur, noblesce, beneurté, richesce, grant humilité*, vv. 1731–4).

⁶⁶ 1737–88: these lines are an addition, perhaps modelled on the similar, though not identical, description of the heavenly court in the Anselmian dialogue *De custodia interioris hominis* (ed. R. W. Southern and F. S. Schmitt, *Memorials of St Anselm*, Auctores Britannici Medii Aevi 1 (London: Oxford University Press for the British Academy, 1969), pp. 354–60; henceforth *De custodia*, referred to by page and line number). This dialogue was given several vernacular translations in medieval England: see R. M. Wilson, *Sawles Warde*, Leeds Studies and Monographs 3 (Leeds: T. Wilson for the School of English Language, University of Leeds, 1938), prints two early Middle English versions). In *De custodia*, as in Clemence's text, the virgin is named next after God, receiving the angels' worship beside her son (*De custodia*, 358/17–19, cf. v. 1768), and before the martyrs (*De custodia*, 358/35–6; cf. vv. 1775–6). The confessors are mentioned with special reference to the apostles and doctors of the church (*De custodia*, 359/2; cf. vv. 1777–8); the heavenly choir of virgins completes the ranks of heaven (*De custodia*, 359/9; cf. vv. 1779–80). See pp. 95–7 below.

⁶⁷ 1745–68: in an addition without equivalent in the Latin source, the Virgin is celebrated in a series of characteristic Marian images (see R. T. Davies, 'Types and Titles of the Blessed Virgin Mary', in his *Medieval English Lyrics* (London: Faber and Faber, 1963), pp. 371–8). As noted by Batt (p. 110), these images are common to Anglo-Norman lyrics and to narratives of the Virgin, as they are to their Middle English counterparts. Included among them is the commonly found metaphor of the Virgin as flower (cf. Isaiah's prophecy of the shoot and flower from the rod of Jesse: Isaiah 11:1). As Batt points out (n. 41), it is also used in Wace's *Conception Nostre Dame* (v. 713). Here it is extended to pick up the theme of Christ as fruit (v. 1753; cf. vv. 965–1000).

⁶⁸ 1773–4: Clemence's distinctly courtly companies of 'young men and noble knights' (AN *bachelerie* and *chevalerie*) have no equivalent in *De custodia*'s troop of blessed martyrs (*De custodia*, 358/36). See also v. 2274.

⁶⁹ 1790–2: see I Corinthians 2:9 (quoted in *Vulgate*, 185/791–2).

⁷⁰ 1847–8: the phrase 'as their bridegroom and lover' (AN *cum lur*

espus e lur ami) is not in the *Vulgate*. On the choir of virgins, see notes
to vv. 581–2 and 1625–30.

[71] 1851: at this point in the Latin source it is God, not specifically
Christ, who visits Catherine (*Vulgate*, 186/825). See also v. 1859.

[72] 1946: presumably, as noted by MacBain (1946n.), a reference to
Constantine. See note to v. 61.

[73] 1991–2000: as Savage and Watson point out (p. 428 n. 38) with
regard to a later speech by Catherine (vv. 2537ff. in Clemence's
translation), Christ is a model for Catherine here, since he reprimands
those who mourn him on the route to the crucifixion and tells them to
weep for themselves (Luke 23:27–8). The accompanying account of the
flesh's transience has its source in the *Vulgate* (190/905–8).

[74] 2061–76: these lines follow the Latin in their content (see *Vulgate*,
192/945–8), but their presentation as a narrative voice's comment and
explication has no equivalent.

[75] 2165–2230: these lines elaborate a much shorter speech in the
Vulgate, borrowing from the conventions of courtly love complaint to
do so. As has long been noted, they recall *Tristan* and other courtly
lovers. See M. Dominica Legge, *Anglo-Norman Literature and its
Background* (Oxford: Clarendon Press, 1963; repr. Westport, Conn.:
Greenwood Press, 1978) pp. 67–8, for a parallel between vv. 2175–6
and Thomas's *Tristan*, and Batt (n. 2) for a parallel between vv.
2175–6 and Tristan's speech in Marie de France's *Chevrefoil*, vv. 77–8.
Batt (n. 64) also provides parallels between vv. 2195–6 and medieval
love lyrics. On Clemence and *Tristan* see Duncan Robertson, 'Writing
in the Textual Community: Clemence of Barking's Life of St. Catherine', *French Forum* 21 (1996), 5–28.

[76] 2231–56: these lines more closely follow the latter part of Maxentius' speech in the *Vulgate*, though without specifically mentioning
Roman women (*Vulgate*, 195/993–1003).

[77] 2263–4: there is no equivalent in the *Vulgate* for the terms by which
the queen here spiritually inverts her social relation to Catherine. The
saint becomes 'royal' (AN *real pulcele*, v. 2263) and the queen becomes
the 'handmaid of God' (AN *Deu ancele*, v. 2264), a term often used of
consecrated young women and nuns (see *Lawrence*, v. 76).

[78] **2277**: AN *barnilment* ('nobly, manfully') translates the Latin source's *uiriliter age*, 'act courageously [*lit.* manfully]' (*Vulgate*, 196/1014).

[79] **2290–6**: Clemence elaborates the promise of an immortal spouse (*Vulgate*, 196/1015) with a fivefold repetition of the theme of sweetness (AN *duçur*, 'sweetness, gentleness': *duz* 2291, *douz* 2292, *duçur* 2293, *endulci* 2294, *douçur* 2296), which has no equivalent in the Latin. Christ's sweetness is a common motif in treatments of Christ as lover, found, as Batt remarks (p. 113 and n. 61), in the vernacular Song of Songs as well as in lyric and devotional prose.

[80] **2313**: as MacBain points out (note to v. 2641), the dates do not fit (either in the Latin or in the vernacular versions). In Clemence's version, the queen's martyrdom on the twenty-third of the month cannot be reconciled with the date of the philosophers' martyrdom (13 November, v. 1151). Catherine is starved in the dungeon for twelve days and visited by the queen on the thirteenth day (v. 1510), interrogated by Maxentius the following morning (v. 1868–74) and then threatened with wheels which take three days to make (v. 2055). This should make the date of the queen's death no earlier than 29 November.

[81] **2317–18**: there is no equivalent for this narratorial comment in the Latin source.

[82] **2335–54**: this account of courtly and hierarchical mourning for the queen is an addition to the *Vulgate*, which narrates only Maxentius' interrogation at this point (*Vulgate*, 1196/1026ff.). Batt (p. 112 and n. 57) compares these lines with the mourning for Tristan in the Anglo-Norman romance by Thomas (*Le Roman de Tristan* ed. Félix Lecoy, CFMA (Paris: Champion, 1991), p. 114, vv. 3043–7).

[83] **2411–30**: these lines expand the Latin source considerably, using the conventions of courtly-love soliloquy and complaint to do so (cf. vv. 2203–18).

[84] **2464–5**: Thursday as the day of the soldiers' execution follows in sequence, since the queen has been killed on a Wednesday, but the actual date is irreconcilable with those earlier given (see note to v. 2313).

[85] **2513–30**: in the Latin source the crowd of mourners is simply composed of 'many men and women' (*Vulgate*, 200/1096). Clemence

again elaborates a hierarchical courtly crowd (see also vv. 2335–54 and note).

[86] 2537–50: as Savage and Watson suggest (see note to vv. 1991–2000 above), the ultimate source for the saint's speech here may be Christ's speech to the women of Jerusalem on the route to Calvary, Luke 23:27–8.

[87] 2622: in the *Vulgate* there is no equivalent for this sentence of narratorial intervention.

[88] 2634: on the eleventh-century 'rediscovery' of Catherine's tomb, see Introduction, pp. xxi–xxii, and C. W. Jones, 'The Norman Cults of St Nicholas and St Catherine saec. xi', in *Hommages à André Boutemy*, Collection Latomus 145 (Brussels, 1976), pp. 216–30; repr. in C. W. Jones, *St Nicholas of Myra, Bari, and Manhattan: Biography of a Legend* (Chicago and London: University of Chicago Press, 1978), pp. 144–54. Clemence omits the *Vulgate*'s claim that Mount Sinai is twenty and more days' journey from the place of Catherine's martyrdom (*Vulgate*, 202/1139–203/1140), and its mention of the tiny bone fragments which sometimes flow out with the oil from Catherine's shrine (*Vulgate*, 203/1143–4).

[89] 2639–40: this sentence has no equivalent in the *Vulgate* and is again part of Clemence's creation of an oral narrative persona.

[90] 2641–3: the date of Catherine's feast, 25 November, is correctly given, though the chronology of the narrative action is askew in both the Latin source and the vernacular versions (see note to v. 2313). Because Friday is the day of the crucifixion, it is specially appropriate that Catherine's martyrdom, rather than the queen's or Porphiry's, should occur on it.

[91] 2647–88: these lines have no equivalent in the Latin source, which moves from the Christ-like hour of Catherine's death directly to its closing formula (*Vulgate*, 203/1147–8). In Clemence's text links recalling the prologue (see especially vv. 3, 9, 20) are made between God's goodness (AN *bunté*, vv. 2654, 2676, 2685), human goodwill (AN *bon voleir*, v. 2648; *bone volenté*, v. 2650; *volenté*, v. 2686) and God's inexhaustible love and desire for humans to love and desire him (vv. 2651–2, 2661, 2679–80).

[92] **2691**: on Barking, a major Benedictine nunnery, see Introduction, pp. xxiv–xxvii.

St Lawrence

References to the Anglo-Norman text of the *Life of St Lawrence* are by line number to the edition by D. W. Russell, *La Vie de saint Laurent: An Anglo-Norman Poem of the Twelfth Century*, ANTS 34 (London: ANTS, 1976). References to the chief Latin source of *Lawrence* are by page and paragraph number to the edition by H. Delehaye, 'Recherches sur le légendier romain', *Analecta Bollandiana*, 51 (1933), 72–98 (hereafter *Passion*).

[1] **1–2**: the narrator's appeal as pupil to master (*maistre*) for help in correcting the translation (v. 16) has a close parallel in Philippe de Thaon's *Cumpoz*, vv. 161–80. See Russell, note to v. 1; *Der Computus*, ed. Eduard Mall (Strasbourg: Trübner, 1873), vv. 161–80. On Anglo-Norman prologues, see the works listed in *Catherine*, note to vv. 1–50.

[2] **4–14**: see Ecclesiasticus 12:8–9. As Russell notes, Jesus the son of Sirach (*c.* 200 BC) was the author of Ecclesiasticus, originally written in Greek and translated into Hebrew by the author's grandson. A similar proverbial saying is used in *Catherine* (see note to vv. 1031–2); cf. Schulze-Busacker, *Proverbes*, no. 70: 'Au besoing voit on l'ami'.

[3] **15–18**: as in *Catherine*, vv. 35–46 (and see note to vv. 35–46) textual processes occasion ethical reflection on transience and decay. It is possible that the notion of making a mistake (v. 17, AN *mesdire*) has moral and not merely technical connotations here.

[4] **19–58**: an elaboration of mutability and transience topoi, which supports *Lawrence*'s theme of the impermanence of worldly treasures versus the enduring reality of good deeds. In the psalm with which Lawrence is specially associated (see note to vv. 154–7), it is said that the righteous man and his generosity will be remembered for ever (Psalms 112:6, 9). Cf. St Catherine's account to Porphiry of the mutability and uncertainty of life by contrast to the joys of the heavenly city (*Catherine*, vv. 1667–96).

[5] **29–32**: Ecclesiastes 1:1 names its author as the son of David. For vv. 31–2, see Ecclesiastes 1:10.

⁶ 38–42: this list was often used in the twelfth century in 'ubi sunt' laments on transience, most influentially by Honorius of Autun in his *Elucidarium* (which follows Anselm in *Proslogion*, ch. 25). See G. Shepherd, '"All the wealth of Croesus ...": A Topic in the *Ancrene Riwle*', *Modern Language Review*, 51 (1956), 161–7.

⁷ 76: on possible identities and contexts for the handmaiden of St Lawrence, see Introduction, p. xxxviii. The Anglo-Norman term *ancele* (from Latin *ancilla*, 'handmaiden') has usually been taken to indicate a nun as the commissioner of *Lawrence* (see Russell, note to v. 76). A laywoman with a special devotion to the saint would not, however, be an impossible alternative.

⁸ 93–4: as Russell points out (pp. 24–5), in this introductory section on Sixtus (Pope Sixtus II, martyred AD 258) the material of the Latin legend is re-arranged and condensed. Details from other, abridged versions of the *Passion of Polychronius* are also introduced, such as Sixtus' awareness of Decius' arrival in Rome (Russell, p. 24). In the *Passion*, Decius and his prefect Valerianus simply command Sixtus and his clergy to their tribunal at Tellus, and the pope has no prior warning (*Passion*, 80/11). The Anglo-Norman writer has thus taken some care to introduce events from the point of view of the martyred clerics.

⁹ 95: the legend confuses the persecution of Decius (Roman emperor AD 249–51) with that of Valerian (emperor AD 253–59/60), by whose edict Lawrence and Sixtus were martyred in AD 258 (Russell, 95n. and 96–102nn.). See Delehaye, pp. 43–4 and 49–50. In his influential later thirteenth-century *Legenda aurea*, Jacobus de Voragine, archbishop of Genoa (d. 1298), assembles and reviews major sources for Lawrence's legend and attempts to resolve discrepancies. He states that 'sometimes in antiquity, some emperors were made *Caesares* but not *Augusti*, or emperors in the full sense.... At the time of the emperors Valerian and Gallienus, Sixtus occupied the see of Rome. Therefore, this Decius Caesar, so called, who subjected blessed Laurence to martyrdom, was not made an emperor and is never called *Decius imperator*, but only *Decius Caesar*, in the legend of Saint Laurence' (*Jacobus de Voragine, The Golden Legend: Readings on the Saints*, trans. William Granger Ryan (Princeton, NJ: Princeton University Press, 1993), II, p. 67). In the earlier part of the Latin legend, Decius is said to have

martyred Polychronius in a persecution in Persia. He then brings back and martyrs two Christian princes, Abdon and Sennen, before arresting Sixtus (*Passion*, 72/1–80/10).

[10] 125–7: in the *Passion*, Lawrence is not introduced until after Sixtus' arrest and is described only as the archdeacon of Sixtus (*Passion*, 81/13). The account of Lawrence's birth and accomplishments in vv. 126–7 is an addition by the Anglo-Norman writer.

[11] 128: in the early church bishops selected one of their seven deacons to help in divine service (see vv. 225–6) and in administration. The archdeacon often succeeded the bishop in the bishopric, and Lawrence, appropriately enough, succeeds Sixtus in martyrdom. As dioceses grew larger in the Western church, several archdeacons were often necessary. By the twelfth century, for instance, the diocese of Lincoln had seven. Archdeacons had become very powerful with quasi-episcopal status, but this was curbed after the twelfth century (W. E. Addis and T. Arnold, *A Catholic Dictionary*, rev. T. B. Scannell (London: Virtue & Co., 1893; 11th edition, 1928), *s.v.* 'archdeacon'.

[12] 132–40: Lawrence's question (repeated at v. 224) and Sixtus' reply occur in the *Passion* after Sixtus' arrest and before the treasures are entrusted to Lawrence (*Passion*, 82/13). Medieval liturgies in England quoted the wording of this question in the offices for the Vigil, Feast and Octave of St Lawrence (9, 10 and 17 August respectively). For a listing of this and other liturgical uses of Lawrence's legend, see Ziolkowski, Appendix II, pp. 245–7.

[13] 141–4: these lines have no equivalent in the Latin source, where Sixtus' promise that Lawrence will follow him after three days is not commented on as a miracle (*Passion*, 82/13). In the *Passion* Sixtus uses the scriptural title for a deacon (Latin *levita*; see Cabrol and Leclercq, VIII, pt 2 (1929), cols 2992–3, and *ODCC*, p. 819, *s.v.* 'levite'). This term is never translated or commented on in the Anglo-Norman text, where in vv. 127–8 Lawrence is named only as a 'deacon' (*diacnes*) and archdeacon (*archidiacnes*).

[14] 147–50: in the *Passion* Lawrence confides the vestments and treasures to the widow Cyriaca, who has been sheltering many Christians and clergy in her house, and he cures her of an ailment (*Passion*, 83/14). In the abbreviated Latin versions of the legend, Lawrence is

said to sell the treasures to Christian craftsmen (perhaps to goldsmiths and silversmiths?) rather than to give them away. See Russell, p. 25 n. 44 and note to v. 150. Presumably this is so that the treasures can be turned into alms for the poor who are mentioned in v. 151.

[15] **156-7**: a single word quoted in Latin (*dispersit*, 'he distributed', v. 156) suffices to invoke Psalm 111 (112):9–10: 'He distributed, he gave to the poor. His generosity (*munificentia*, 112:9: *iustitia*, 'righteousness', 111:9) will endure for ever'. Verse 9 was particularly associated with Lawrence and was extensively used, as Tavormina points out, in the offices for the saint's Vigil, Feast and Octave (M. Teresa Tavormina, '*Piers Plowman* and the Liturgy of St Lawrence: Composition and Revision in Langland's Poetry', *Studies in Philology*, 84 (1987), 245–71 (pp. 259–60). See also Ziolkowski, p. 247. Verse 156 is the first of a number of occasions on which a word or phrase in Latin appears in the French text. See also vv. 241–2, 305, 306, 364, 367, 645, 666, 691, 724, 873, 899, 924, 928, 929, 933, 939.

[16] **165**: in the Anglo-Norman text, the expression *membres Deu* ('followers of God', v. 165) has something of the connotations of the Pauline body and the communion of Christ (I Corinthians 12:12).

[17] **157-68**: the vernacular life omits several scenes from the *Passion*, in which Lawrence, weeping, washes the feet of Christians in houses and cellars, cures the blind man Crescentius, and is joined by the priest Justinus (*Passion*, 83/15–84/16).

[18] **169-242**: in the *Passion*, the first stage of Sixtus' encounter with Decius follows immediately after the cry of Felicissimus and Agapitus (*Passion*, 81/11–12). Sixtus confides the treasures to Lawrence when visited by him in prison, and is subsequently brought before Decius for a second time, interrogated and executed (*Passion*, 84/17–85/18). In the vernacular text, the two scenes between Sixtus and Decius are compressed, the first being amalgamated at the beginning of the second. The junior deacons' cry (vv. 123–4) is directly followed by a scene in which Sixtus entrusts the treasures to Lawrence. In this part of the narrative, the Anglo-Norman text rearranges the material more extensively than when dealing with Lawrence's own passion. Sixtus' contempt for pagan idols (vv. 179–83) and his partial destruction of the temple of Mars (vv. 214–15) remain prominent in the rearrangement, though the role of the junior deacons (sent to prison with Sixtus in the

Passion, 81/12) almost entirely disappears in favour of the vernacular text's concentration on Lawrence and Sixtus.

[19] 182–3: Sixtus' charge that the idols are of gold and silver seems to be an addition in the Anglo-Norman text. It is not present in the *Passion*, where the charges are that the idols are deaf, dumb, unable to help others or themselves and made of stone (*Passion*, 81/12 and 85/17).

[20] 198–202: the Anglo-Norman text expands on the theme of Sixtus' age (cf. *Passion*, 84/17).

[21] 205: the chief Roman temple of Mars, the god of war, was near the Augustan forum, and was used for ceremonies, courts and an annual dedication festival. The twelfth-century *Marvels of Rome* (*Mirabilia urbis Romae*), however, locates Sixtus' martyrdom at a different temple of Mars, outside the Appian Gate, in the modern 'district of San Lorenzo' (Russell, Index of Proper Names, *s.v.* 'Martis'). For a text of *The Marvels of Rome*, see *Der Topographie der Stadt Rom im Alterthum*, ed. H. Jordan (Berlin: Weidmannsche Buchhandlung, 1871), Bd 2, 'Mirabilia Romae', pp. 605–43 (trans. F. M. Nichols, *The Marvels of Rome*, London: Ellis and Elvey, 1889).

[22] 224–6: the Anglo-Norman text has already used Lawrence's cry to Sixtus (at vv. 132–3) and it repeats it here before continuing with Lawrence's account of the eucharistic duties of the principal deacon (vv. 225–6). In the *Passion* the two occasions form a single earlier scene (*Passion*, 82/13). On the duties of deacons, see notes to vv. 128 and 246.

[23] 236: the two junior deacons, Felicissimus and Agapitus, are mentioned at vv. 121–2.

[24] 238–42: the Anglo-Norman narrative condenses and modifies the Latin source. There, Sixtus and the deacons are buried in different cemeteries and there is no mention of a church being founded (*Passion*, 85/18). In the seventh and eighth centuries pilgrims are recorded as visiting the church in the cemetery near the Via Appia 'where St Sixtus was beheaded, together with his deacons' ('Einsiedler Itinerar', ed. Jordan, *Topographie der Stadt Rom im Alterthum*, Bd 2, pp. 658–9). In the Anglo-Norman text, the formula at vv. 241–2 is left in Latin. The same formula is used at this point in one variant text

of the *Passion* (B. Mombritius, *Sanctuarium, seu Vitae sanctorum*, rev. ed. by the monks of Solesme (Paris: Fontemoing, 1910), vol. 2, p. 651), so was possibly in the copy of the text used by the Anglo-Norman writer.

[25] **246**: the duties of an archdeacon (see note to v. 128) included managing church property and providing for the support of the clergy, the poor, widows, prisoners and orphans (Addis and Arnold, *Catholic Dictionary*, *s.v.* 'archdeacon').

[26] **260**: the traditions of the legend vary concerning the provenance of this treasure, just as they vary concerning the exact logic of Lawrence's disposal of it (see note to vv. 147–50). In one version of the passions of Sixtus and Lawrence, Decius is said to have murdered and usurped his way to empire by killing the Emperor Philip in Verona. His son, also named Philip, confides his father's treasure to Sixtus for safe-keeping, before himself being slain by Decius. When Decius returns to Rome, bringing Abdon and Sennen with him (see note to v. 95 above), he seeks Philip's treasure (*Golden Legend*, trans. Ryan, pp. 63–4). In the *Passion* on which *Lawrence* is based, Decius tries to get treasure from two Christian noblemen after he has had Abdon and Sennen killed (*Passion*, 76/5). He is thus, in any version of the treasure's provenance, to be thought of as covetous and so the opposite to Lawrence. In the *Legenda aurea*, James of Voragine comments: 'Do not let it bother you that the treasure which blessed Laurence dispensed is not called the emperor's, but the Church's, because it might well be that he did dispense some of the Church's wealth along with that of Emperor Philip; or perhaps the distributed wealth is called the Church's in view of the fact that Philip had left it to the Church to be given to the poor' (*Golden Legend*, trans. Ryan, II, p. 64). Ziolkowski, p. 62, suggests the contemporary twelfth-century relevance of Nigel of Canterbury's Latin verse version of Lawrence's legend for matters of church ownership and the disposition of church property: 'The courage and triumph of Lawrence in the face of cruel and greedy authorities would have endowed the *passio* with special relevance for a monk who believed that he and his brothers were engaged in a saint-like struggle to protect their rights and possessions from the grasp of a corrupt king and archbishop [Henry II and Archbishop Baldwin, who were trying to establish a college of secular canons at Canterbury].'

[27] **263–4:** this comment on Lawrence's motive is an addition to the Latin source (*Passion*, 86/19).

[28] **266:** Valerian, presented as Decius' provost (*praefectus, Passion*, 80/11), was historically the emperor whose edict sentenced Sixtus and Lawrence to immediate execution as Christian clergy (see note to v. 95).

[29] **287:** for blindness through tears, see Psalms 6:7–8. Lucillus' name (cf. Latin *lux*, 'light') suggests that he will be spiritually enlightened, as indeed proves to be the case.

[30] **293–318:** in the Latin source, Lawrence takes Lucillus through several different articles of the Creed when baptizing him (*Passion*, 86/20–87/20). The Anglo-Norman writer shortens this scene, but then adds further details. Not only do other blind people come flocking but also paralysed and hydroptic people (vv. 305–6). These latter are not mentioned in the *Passion* (87/20).

[31] **305–6:** the terms *paralitici* and *ydropici* are perhaps left in Latin to evoke either the register of medical terminology or that of the Gospel and the Acts of the Apostles (as in Luke 14:2, Acts 8:7).

[32] **313–18:** this prayer is an addition made by the Anglo-Norman writer.

[33] **333–53:** there is no equivalent for these lines in the narration of Lawrence's conversion of Hippolytus in the Latin source (*Passion*, 87/21), but see note to vv. 364–9.

[34] **344:** see Romans 8:31.

[35] **349–53:** See Matthew 10:18–19; Mark 13:9–11; Luke 21:12–15. This quotation is not present in the Latin source. It is also used in *Catherine* (see note to vv. 539–44).

[36] **364–9:** The first word of the Creed (*credo*, 'I believe') is given in Latin in the Anglo-Norman text (cf. *Pater*, note to v. 899). Hippolytus' conversion and baptism are given here with the kind of detail omitted from the Anglo-Norman text's account of Lucillus' baptism (vv. 290–302). Threefold immersion (vv. 368–9) is mentioned in neither baptism in the Latin source, though Lucillus is asked for his belief in each person of the Trinity by name (*Passion* 86/20–87/20).

[37] **376–80:** these lines have no equivalent in the Latin source. Like the narrative persona pervasively created in *Catherine* (see Introduction, pp. xxxii–xxxiii), they inscribe an audience as present and listening.

[38] **408:** the Anglo-Norman narrative particularly emphasizes that the poor have eaten, a detail not present in the *Passion*. They thus both are, and have consumed, the treasure of the church sold by Lawrence on their behalf (see Introduction pp. xli–xlii).

[39] **411–12:** the location of this seat is unspecified in the Anglo-Norman text, but is named in the Latin source as the palace of Sallust (*Passion*, 88/22), not mentioned until v. 765 in *Lawrence*.

[40] **418–19:** these lines are a close translation of the *Passion* ('isti sunt thesauri aeterni, qui numquam minuuntur et semper crescunt', *Passion*, 88/22) and also appear in the York *Breviary* (col. 464, see Ziolkowski, p. 246). There is no exact scriptural source, but many verses on treasure have similar themes. See Matthew 6:20, 13:44, 19:21; Mark 10:21; Luke 18:22 (cited Ziolkowski, p. 146, note to vv. 1443–4).

[41] **435:** the mention of precious metals has no equivalent in the *Passion*. It echoes Sixtus' earlier characterization of the idols (v. 183).

[42] **443–515:** Decius' question becomes the occasion of a major expansion in the Anglo-Norman text. Only the question itself (v. 443) is taken direct from the Latin source (*Passion*, 88/22). In vv. 444–63, Lawrence develops the themes of his previous speech (vv. 430–41) by still more intense word-play contrasting God's creation and human manufacture of idols (*creature*, 448, 452; *cria*, 462; *crié*, 461; *fait*, 445–8, 451, 454–6, 459, 463; *fist*, 457, 463; *faiture*, 447, 453; see pp. 100–101 below). This theme is also treated in *Catherine* (see vv. 209–16). In vv. 466–515 Lawrence responds to a second question by a compact exposition of salvation history, using similar themes and word-play to that of *Catherine* (see note to *Catherine*, vv. 965–1000).

[43] **458–9:** Psalms 32 (33):9 (on the theme of God's creation, see Psalms 35 (36):7; 73 (74):15; 148:10). The reference to the psalter may constitute an allusion to texts with which the 'handmaiden of St Lawrence' (v. 76) can be assumed to be familiar. The psalter would have been standard reading for both lay and professed women in the twelfth century. See further the works cited in *Catherine*, note to vv. 141–4.

[44] **480–3:** like *Catherine* (see vv. 724–6, 1745–68), *Lawrence*'s added lines on the Virgin draw on stock Marian epithets, though from sources different from those of *Catherine*. Vv. 482–3 are close to the Marian prayer *Obsecro te* ('I beseech you'), which, though rare in psalters, became widespread in books of hours (see Roger S. Wieck, *The Book of Hours in Medieval Art and Life* (London: Sotheby's Publications, 1988), pp. 163–4; and V. Leroquais, *Les Livres d'heures manuscrits de la Biblothèque Nationale* (Paris: by subscription, 1927), II, 346, no. xxxviii. See also, for an example in vernacular lyric, *The Anglo-Norman Lyric*, ed. Jeffery and Levy, nos. 9A and 9B.

[45] **494–507:** see *Catherine*, note to vv. 965–1000.

[46] **519–23:** in the Latin source Lawrence is beaten 'with whips' (*scorpionibus*, *Passion*, 88:23). The Anglo-Norman text's thorns (*aiglanter*, 'wild rose branches', v. 519) may reflect medieval imagery of Christ's passion (cf. Bohort's vision of Lionel in the Grail Quest, naked, beaten with thorns, and bleeding copiously from 'more than a hundred places, so that he was covered with blood front and back': see *La Queste del Saint Graal*, ed. A. Pauphilet, CFMA 33 (Paris: Champion, 1923; repr. 1984), p. 175, vv. 7–11). Thorns were also used in penitential disciplinary practices: in an early thirteenth-century *Guide for Anchoresses*, the female recipients are warned not to beat themselves with holly or thorns without their confessor's permission. The anchoresses are also warned against the use of lead-weighted scourges such as are used on Lawrence (vv. 666–9): see B. Millett and J. Wogan-Browne, *Medieval English Prose for Women* (Oxford: Oxford University Press, repr. 1992), p. 136/15–16.

[47] **540–3:** the Anglo-Norman writer paraphrases a list of torture instruments, named in the *Passion* as *lamminae ferreae et lecti et plumbatae et cardi* ('plates of iron, beds, leaded scourges and wire-toothed brushes', *Passion*, 89/23).

[48] **555:** the Latin gives *epulas*, 'dishes of food' (*Passion*, 89/23). The Anglo-Norman *viande* used in this line can mean 'food, a dish of food, sustenance, meat' (*AND, s.v.* 'viande').

[49] **558:** Decius uses the Christian term *escumengé* 'excommunicated'.

[50] **568:** perhaps a reference to the open 'book of life' in Revelation 20:12, in which the names of the saved were believed to be written.

[51] **633:** it is not clear what, if any, source is represented by this line. Since the *Passion* describes the *lamminas* of v. 631 as made of iron and burning hot (*laminas ferreas ardentes*) and Decius commands them to be applied to Lawrence's sides (*Passion*, 89/24), the reference to the Romans in v. 633 may have been invented to give authority to the Anglo-Norman writer's own explication of *laminas*.

[52] **642–5:** as Russell notes (p. 67, note to v. 645) these lines have not been taken direct from the Latin source (*accusatus non negavi, interrogatus te dominum confessus sum*, *Passion*, 89:24). The Latin formula in v. 645 closely resembles the profession of faith before baptism in Acts 8:37, and the phrase *Iesum Christum, filium Dei* occurs earlier in the Latin source as part of Lucillus' profession of faith when Lawrence baptizes him (*Passion*, 86/20).

[53] **666–9:** Unlike the *laminas* of v. 631 this torment is explained without any further authority than that of the narrative voice. In the Latin source, the *plumbatae* are not explained, but once they have been mentioned Lawrence asks God to receive his spirit (*Passion* 90/24–5). The Anglo-Norman equivalent of this speech is reserved until Lawrence has been beaten with *plunbatis* (v. 666) for some time, thus emphasizing his heroism still further.

[54] **691:** in the Latin source Lawrence is said to be 'lying on the catasta' (*prostratus in catasta, Passion*, 90/25) when Decius gives the command translated at v. 689. In the Latin source, this is a command to beat Lawrence with whips again (*scorpionibus, Passion*, 90/25). The Anglo-Norman text does not translate this as 'whips', as on a previous occasion (see vv. 519–23), but has Decius command all forms of torture (v. 689). This leaves open the question as to whether the *catasta* is a form or a place of torture. The word originally referred to a stage or scaffold where slaves were exposed for sale, but also came to mean an instrument of torture and a cage (Latham, *Dictionary of Medieval Latin from British Sources, s.v.* 'catasta'; and Cabrol and Leclercq, II, pt 2 *s.v.* 'catasta'). It was also sometimes conflated with Lawrence's gridiron (as in Nigel Wireker's version (Ziolkowski, v. 1775), where a *catasta* is prepared for beating Lawrence and is later re-used for grilling him (p. 230, note to v. 1775). In illustration the scaffold and the gridiron could look very similar. The Anglo-Norman writer makes them two separate things:

the *catasta* is treated as a particular Roman torture and as a technical term, and Decius orders a bed of iron made like a gridiron (vv. 833–7).

[55] **695:** for the importance of the saint's cheerfulness (also commented on at v. 828), see II Corinthians 9:7, note to vv. 891–3 and Introduction, p. xxxiii.

[56] **707:** in the Latin source, Romanus is said to be a soldier (*Passion*, 90/26). Ziolkowski compares his role in Lawrence's legend with that of Longinus in Christ's passion. Longinus is cured of physical blindness by blood running down the spear with which he wounds Christ. Romanus is cured of spiritual blindness (Ziolkowski, p. 231, note to v. 1825).

[57] **746:** Romanus' feast day is 9 August. See Farmer, *Oxford Dictionary of Saints, s.n.* 'Romanus' (1). Russell (p. 67, note to 746) points out that the fifth calend of August is 28 July in the modern calendar. Dating by the Roman calendar will have seemed less arcane to the handmaiden of St Lawrence (v. 76) or to the nuns in Derby Priory who owned a manuscript of his Anglo-Norman life than it may to a modern reader. It is the standard medieval form, used in the psalter and in books of hours. The work on which the writer of *Lawrence* may have drawn in vv. 1–16 (see note to vv. 1–2) is an Anglo-Norman *Computus* written between 1121 and 1135 by Philippe de Thaon. It explains the calendar and the Roman 'pagan' system of dating and its Christian adaptation (see Legge, *Anglo-Norman Literature and its Background*, pp. 18–22).

[58] **747–9:** there is no equivalent for this prayer in the Latin source.

[59] **751–4:** in the Latin source, Romanus is buried, like Lawrence himself, in the crypt in the field of Veranus (*Passion*, 91/26). The information at v. 753 that Justinus had been ordained by Sixtus is given earlier in the source (*Passion*, 84/16) before the point at which the Anglo-Norman life begins.

[60] **760:** the scene of Lawrence's interrogation has already been shifted to the palace of Tiberius (v. 571), an imperial palace located, as Russell notes (Index of Proper Names, *s.n.* 'Tiberii'), on the Palatine Hill. The inconsistency of the action's now being said to move away from the temple of Jupiter is more apparent than real. In the *Passion*, when Decius commands the previous move to the palace of Tiberius, he also orders the preparation of his own tribunal at the temple of Jupiter

(*Passion*, 89/24). The temple of Jupiter was the principal temple and stood on the Capitoline Hill, the central hill of Rome's seven. Its ruins were still visible in the twelfth century (see Richard Krautheimer, *Rome: Profile of a City, 312–1308* (Princeton, NJ: Princeton University Press, 1980), p. 285).

[61] **761–3:** the baths of Olympias are named several times as the site of Lawrence's torture on the gridiron in interpolations in the twelfth-century pilgrim-guide *The Marvels of Rome* (ed. Jordan, *Topographie der Stadt Rom im Alterthum*, Bd 2, pp. 612, 617). They are said to be located in Panisperna (district of one of the major early Roman churches dedicated to Lawrence, S. Lorenzo in Formoso). It is not certain that the baths existed as such, though they are named in several versions of the Latin legend (see Russell, Index of Proper Names, *s.n.* 'Olimpiadis, termes'; *Passion*, 91/27). There is no equivalent in the Latin source to the comment in vv. 762–3.

[62] **764:** the theatre of Augustus lay between the temple of Jupiter and the palace of Sallust, which stood near the Porta Salaria (near the modern Via Veneto and some distance from the Capitol). As it is, the trajectory of Lawrence's interrogations and torture is extensive. Several districts of ancient and medieval Rome are traversed, suggesting that the legend was designed to include as many as possible of the ancient Roman churches dedicated to Lawrence.

[63] **778–81:** Hippolytus' speech is reminiscent of Lawrence's and the junior deacons' own earlier questions to Sixtus (vv. 123–4, 132–5, 224).

[64] **792–5:** in the Latin source the instruments of torture are listed as *plumbatas, fustes, lamminas, ungues, lectos, batilos* [variant: *batulos*] ('leaded scourges, cudgels, [metal] plates, hooks, [iron?] beds, tongs' *Passion*, 91/27).

[65] **800–7:** in the Latin source Lawrence explains that following his birth in Spain he was brought up in Rome and has learnt both secular and sacred law (*Passion*, 91/27). In the Anglo-Norman text, he gives something closer to the curriculum of a medieval cleric's education, with a foundation in the *trivium* of grammar, logic and rhetoric (cf *Catherine*, vv. 141–4).

[66] **824–5:** perhaps a scriptural echo. See Psalms 138 (139):11–12 and

Revelation 22:5. St Catherine also sees light in the darkness of her dungeon (*Catherine*, vv. 1449–56).

[67] 828: On Lawrence's cheerfulness, see notes to vv. 695, 890–3.

[68] 835–6: although beds have been mentioned earlier in lists of torture instruments in the Latin source (*lecti*, see note to vv. 540–3; *lectos*, note to vv. 792–5), the word *craticula*, 'gridiron', used in some versions to refer to the *catasta* (see note to v. 691), is used for the first time here (*Passion*, 92:28). As Russell points out (836n.), the Anglo-Norman text's equivalent (*gredil*, v. 920, nom. sg. *gerdis*) may owe something to northern English *girdle, griddle*.

[69] 849–50, 853: see Psalms 50 (51):19. In vv. 851–3 the Anglo-Norman author once again uses the psalter as a reference point for the audience (see notes to vv. 458–9, 871–3).

[70] 864–7: as on a previous occasion (see note to vv. 824–5), Lawrence's speech is reminiscent of, though not precisely paralleled in, the use in the liturgy of Psalms 16:3. The Sarum use is less close to the psalm, but among the closest and most appropriate to this moment in the legend: 'On the gridiron, I did not deny you, touched with fire, I acknowledged you' (see Introduction, n. 70 above).

[71] 871–3: as Russell points out (note to vv. 871–3), these lines are close to the Gallican Psalter's version of Psalms 65.11 in the twelfth-century Oxford Psalter (ed. F. X. Michel, *Libri psalmorum versio antiqua gallica* (Oxford: Typographia Academia, 1860), p. 84). The equivalent in the Vulgate Bible (Psalms 65:12) is less close. On the use of the psalter in *Lawrence*, see notes to vv. 458–9, 849–50.

[72] 890–3: the Anglo-Norman author seems to have used both of the major variants in the Latin source. Lawrence is there said to have a 'calm' face in some manuscripts and a 'most beautiful' face in others (*Passion*, 92/28, n.25). On the importance of saints' bodily decorum and composure, see Introduction, pp. xxxiii, and *Catherine*, notes to vv. 595–626, 1183–1238. See also *Lawrence*, vv. 695, 828.

[73] 896–7: the earliest known version of this famous taunt (present in the Latin source, *Passion*, 92/28) is found in the writings of St Ambrose AD 339–97). See Introduction, p. xxxvi.

[74] 899–903: it is not clear why the Anglo-Norman author quotes part

of the salutation to God in Latin, but *pater* could have been assumed to be familiar to any handmaid of St Lawrence (v. 76) as the opening of the *Pater noster* ('Our Father . . .') and from liturgical uses. Russell suggests that one or more lines may have been lost from the text after v. 901 (Russell, note to vv. 896–905).

[75] **924–7:** the Tiburtine Gate is the Roman city gate nearest the field of Veranus. As Russell points out (Index of Proper Names, *s.n.* 'Tiburtina, in'), the gate is still in use, and the cemetery a short distance outside it. The incorporation of Latin phrases is particularly marked in this concluding passage and occurs also in vv. 928–9, 933, 939. The death of the principal martyr of the legend, and the importance of feast and shrine details in saints' cults, perhaps account for these uses of Latin in the concluding passages of the Anglo-Norman text. On the other hand, haste to finish might also explain them.

[76] **928–9:** the widow remains unnamed in the Anglo-Norman text. In the Latin source she is Cyriaca, whom Lawrence had earlier healed. This scene is omitted from the Anglo-Norman text, probably as a consequence of the decision to abridge and clarify the action concerning Sixtus and Lawrence (see note to vv. 147–50). Following state appropriation of Christian cemeteries within the walls of Rome in the second century, martyrs' bodies had to be buried in private Christian cemeteries outside the walls. The church of S. Lorenzo fuori le Mure still stands. It is a double basilica, built by the Emperor Constantine (see Index of Proper Names) over the crypt owned by Cyriaca. The rest of the field of Veranus now forms part of Rome's principal Catholic cemetery. Other ancient churches dedicated to Lawrence in Rome are supposed to have been founded by pious noblewomen, for example, S. Lorenzo in Miranda (Cabrol and Leclercq, XIV, pt 2, col. 2958) and S. Lorenzo in Lucina (ibid., VIII, pt 2, col. 1955).

[77] **933:** Lawrence's feast-day is 10 August. On the use of the Roman calendar, see note to v. 746.

[78] **939:** the Latin phrase used in the Anglo-Norman text for 'communion' is 'the body of Christ' (*Corpus Christi*) and would be a familiar phrase to medieval audiences, including those without Latin. There is no equivalent in the Latin source, which continues with the marytrdom of Hippolytus (*Passion*, 93/30).

APPENDIX

The following passages are representative examples from the original Anglo-Norman texts. Line references correspond to those in the editions used in this volume.

Extracts from The Life of St Catherine

(i) Clemence of Barking's Prologue

    Cil ki le bien seit e entent
    Demustrer le deit sagement,
    Que par le fruit de sa bunté
4 Seient li altre amonesté
    De bien faire e de bien voleir
    Sulunc ço qu'en unt le poeir.
    Car cil ki sul est bon de sei
8 A nus dunad essample e lei;
    Sa bunté ne nus volt celer,
    Mais cumunement demustrer.
    De sun bien suffist chascun
12 Car il sul est a tuz commun.
    De sa grant largesce nus paist
    E tut nostre bien del suen naist.
    Beneurez est ki s'i alie
16 E a cel grant bien sun cuer plie
    Que mueisun de tens ne mue
    Ne lai ne [re]prent ne argue.
    Unkes a nul ne volt failir
20 Ki de lui oust desir.
    Mult ad en li riche cunquest
    Ki tut jurz fud e ert e est.
    Or li preum par sa dolçur

24 Qu'il nus doinst faire tel labur
E issi sivre ici sa trace,
Que la le veum face a face
U il regne en sa majesté
28 Uns Deus en sainte trinité.
Par sa pieté m'en deit aidier
A cel ovre que vuil traitier
D'une sue veraie amie,
32 De qui voil translater la vie,
De latin respundre en rumanz
Pur ço que plus plaise as oianz.
Ele fud jadis translaté
36 Sulunc le tens bien ordené;
Mais ne furent dunc si veisdus
Les humes, ne si envius
Cum il sunt al tens ki est ore
40 E aprés nus serrunt uncore.
Pur ço que li tens est mué
E des humes la qualité
Est la rime vil tenue
44 Car ele est asquans corrumpue.
Pur ço si l'estuet amender
E le tens selunc la gent user.
Ne l'aiment pas pur mun orgoil,
48 Kar preisie estre n'en voil;
Il sul en deit loenge aveir
De qui sai mun povre saveir.

(ii) How could God die? An extract from Catherine's reply to the clerks:

'Jo die que Deu nostre salvere
952 Est par nature uel al pere,
E des qu'il est al pere uel,
Dunc n'est il pas en sei mortel.
Il ne pot en sei mort suffrir,
956 Ne dolur ne peine sentir.
Pur ço que murir ne poeit
En la nature u il esteit,

Se vesti de char e de sanc
960   Qu'il recut d'un virginel flanc.
Sa nature pas ne muad,
Mais nostre par soe honurad.
La sue ne pot estre enpeirie,
964   Mais la nostre par soe essalcie.
Le pere ki lui enveiad,
Ki tute rien de nient furma,
Quant hume e femme aveit crié,
968   De mal de bien poeir duné,
Cist hume par le fruit pechia
Del fust que Deus li deveia.
Par cel fruit fumes nus dampnez
972   E a cruele mort livrez.
Pur ço que Deus ne velt suffrir
Que hume doust issi perir,
Reçut la fraile charn de l'hume
976   Pur guarir le fait de la pume.
Par le fruit del fust deveé
Fud tut le mund a mort livré.
Jesu fud le fruit acetable
980   E a tut le mund feunable.
Icist bon fruit fud en croiz mis,
Si ramenad en pareis
L'ume ki en fu hors geté
984   Par le fruit ki fud deveé.
Par cest froit fume nus guariz
Ki par l'altre fumes periz.'

(iii) Catherine describes the court of heaven:

'En cele grant cité real
Est tut tens li reis nun mortal,
Ki unkes n'ot cumencement
1740   Ne ja n'avra definement,
Le bels, li pius, le glorius,
As chastes amanz deliçus,
La qui vertu tute rien sent,
1744   Mer e tere, quanqu'i apent.

Iluec est la bele reine
Ki ambure est mere e meschine.
Dedenz sun chaste cors porta
1748   Sun bon faitre ki la furma.
Il est sun fiz e sun pere;
Ele est sa fille e sa mere.
De ceste burjuna la flur
1752   Ki tute rien paist de s'odur;
De ceste eissi le bon fruit,
Dunt li fernal sunt destruit.
Ceste dame est sainte Marie;
1756   Mere est al rei ki maintient vie.
De li s'esmerveille nature,
Car unc ne fu tel criature.
Ceste est as dolur[u]s deport;
1760   Ceste est as orphanins cunfort.
En li est la nostre fiance;
A nus est de vie esperance.
Ceste sule est empereriz,
1764   Par qui tut li munz est guariz.
Ceste sule est dame e reine,
A qui tute rien est acline.
En pareis est aluee;
1768   Deled sun fiz siet curunee.
[Iloc est la grant compaignie
Des angles et la melodie.
La est li duz festival chant
1772   Ki tut tenz est uelement grant.]
La est la grant bachelerie
E la noble chevalerie
De seinz martyrs ki mort venquirent,
1776   Ki pur amur Deu la suffrirent.
Li apostle e li bon doctur
I sunt, e li bon confessur.
Le coer i est des dameiseles,
1780   Des virges e des chastes pulceles
Ki les mortels amanz despistrent.
E la chaste amur Deu eslistrent.
Trestuit loent cumunalment

1784   Le nun al rei omnipotent.
       Ami, poi est ço que t'ai dit
       D'icel nun disable delit
       De la joie de parais,
1788   Que Deu pramet a ses amis.
       Mais une rien tres bien te di,
       Que oil ne vit n'oreille n'oi,
       Ne coer ne puet unkes penser,
1792   Ne lenge ne puet recunter
       La grant joie que iloc ad,
       Que Deus a ses feelz dunra.
       Ço purras encore saveir,
1796   Se tu en as parfit voleir.'

(iv) Maxentius mourns his wife's conversion and decides to have her killed:

       'Las, que me valt ore m'amur,
2184   Quant n'i receif el que dulur.
       En grant tristur demenrai ma vie,
       Quant jo vus perdrai, bele amie.
       [Kar sule esteies mun delit,
2188   Et jeo le ten, [si] cum jeo quit.]
       Mais ore sai bien e entent,
       Que surquidance noist suvent;
       Pur ço que tant vus poi amer,
2192   Suleie altel de vus quider;
       Mais bien crei par ceste pruvance,
       Que el ne fud fors surquidance.
       [Chaitifs ore sui, tut deceu,
2196   Mort et trai et confundeu.
       Or n'arai mais nul reconfort;
       Or ne desir el que la mort.
       Mei ne purra [ja] rien guarir,
2200   Kant le plus pert de mun desir;
       Et quant li plus averai perdeu,
       De[l] meins serrai puis susteneu?]
       Poi me valdra [puis] mun poeir,
2204   Quant perdu avrai mun voleir;

[Kar desque mun voleir me faut,
De ceo ke ne voil, mei ke chaut?]
Quel joie purrai jo aveir
2208   De poissance cuntre voleir?
[Las, tut puis ceo ke ne ruis,
Et ceo ke plus voil, pas ne puis.]
Cuntre voleir poeir acoil,
2212   Mais cest voleir senz poeir doil.
Car si jo en usse poissance,
Dunc fust fenie ma grevance.
Ore ne sai jo a quel fin traire,
2216   Quant [jo] mun voleir ne pois faire,
[N'a quele cure mun quer juenge,
Kant tute honur de mei s'esluinge.]
Jo en serrai mult avilé
2220   E des miens [le] meins reduté,
Que ma femme issi me hunist
E pur tel folur me guerpist,
[Jeo ki sui reis et emperere
2224   Et de cest regne guvernere,
Si dei cristiens justiser
Et faire lur fol entente laissier.
Ore unt les mens si enganez,
2228   Ke tuz mes deus unt avilez.]
Cument m'en purrai cunseillier
De la tolte de ma moiller?
[Si me destreint si nostre amur,
2232   Que ne venge cest folur,]
Ces altres dames, que ferunt?
Par fei, a li essample prendrunt,
Si enganerunt lur segnurs,
2236   Qu'il crerrunt en ces errurs.
De dous mals deit l'um al mielz traire.
Mielz m'avient justise faire,
Que pur la folie de li
2240   Seit tut le mien regne peri.
[Meuz voil destreindre mun curage,
Ke tuz eient pur mei damage.]
'Dame, fait il, pur ço te di,

2244   E einz la menace te pri,
       Que tu laisses ceste folie
       Dunt tu iés malement perie,
       U si ço nun, jo t'ocirai,
2248   Car nul plus bel cunseil ne sai.
       [Mes de ceo ne te joiras mie,
       Ke ta peine seit par mort finie,
       Kar ge te toudrai cest confort,
2252   Que n'averas hastive mort.]
       A tun oés sai peines nuveles;
       Del piz t'esturterai les mameles,
       Pois de doins cungié de murir,
2256   Si te grant ta mort esjoir.'

(v) Catherine goes to execution:

       Ki dunc veist icele dulur,
2512   Pur nient demandereit majur.
       Mainte face i out arusee
       E meinte voiz en halt criee.
       Meint bel oil i out moillié
2516   E maint suspir fait de pitié.
       Li viel, li jofne, plurent tuit;
       A tuz est comun cel deduit.
       Li riche plaient sa noblesce
2520   E li povre sa grant largesce.
       Li gentil plaient sun parage
       E la rascaille sun domage.
       Les dames plaient sa belté,
2524   Sun sens e sa deboneirité.
       Ki veist ces nobles meschines
       Plurer e batre lur peitrines!
       Plaient la bele Cateline
2528   Cume lur cumpaine et lur veisine.
       Ço ert lur greinur entente
       De pleindre sa bele juvente.
       Mais unc ne puet estre flechie
2532   Pur cumpaine ne pur amie.
       Ele se reguarde a itant,

Veit la gent ki la vait siwant.
Les dames prent a cunforter,
2536	Pur ço qu'ele les veit plurer.
'Ohi, fait ele, gentils pulceles,
E vus, nobles barnesses beles,
Pur Deu vus pri, ne me plainiez,
2540	Ne de ma mort pitié n'aiez.
Se ço est natural pitié
U charité u amistié,
Se vus esjoissiez od mei,
2544	Kar ja m'apele mun bon rei,
Le mien espus, le mien ami,
En qui sur tute rien m'afi.
Ces plurs que vus pur mei perdez,
2548	Sur vus meimes, pri, les turnez,
Que Deu vus gette d'icest' errur,
Einz que viengiez al derein jur.'

Extracts from The Life of St Lawrence

(i) Pagan idols versus God the Creator.

Saint Lorenz dit al mescreable:
'Ohi, tu, membre de deable,
A quei dis tu que crestien
432	Aort deable cumme paen?
Nen est lei que crestien aort
Tel deu qui est mu et sort,
Car d'or sunt, d'argent et d'araim,
436	Et si sunt sort, mu, et vain.
Sainte Escripture idles les nunme
Car faiture sunt de main d'unme;
Or soit sus vous le jugement;
440	Quel doit aorer tote gent,
Ou ceo qu'om fait ou cil quis fait?
Decius dit: 'Ceo cunment vait?
Ki est qui fait, et k'om fait qui?'
444	Lorenz dit: 'Ton deu que vei ici

Est ceo qu'om fait, et ne fait rien,
Car il ne fait ne mal ne bien.
Il est fait cumme faiture;
448 Ceo que fait est, la creature
Ne doit par raison aorer,
Ne son Creator aviler.
Car quant ceo que l'en fait aore,
452 Sei avile, car creature
Est plus haute que faiture.
Ouevre d'alcun est ceo qu'en fait,
Mais Deu fait tot, par lui tot vait.
456 Il est qui fait, car tote ovraigne
Fist es sis jors de la semaine,
Cum el salter trovun estcrit
Que tot fu fait des qu'il out dit;
460 Tresque son plesir out mandé
Si fu quanque est, ou fu, crié.
Qui tot cria par ceo qu'il dist,
Est qui fait, car tot de nient fist.'

(ii) Debate and torture en route to the gridiron.

Et saint Lorenz lui respundi:
'Veirs est, en mun tresor m'afi
604 Que nule peour n'ai de tei.
En cil m'afi en qui jeo crei.
En mon tresor ai esperance
Que tei ne dot ne ta faisance.
608 Crei al tresor celestien
Que ne dout torment terrien.
Ne l'avras ja par nul torment;
Doné l'ai tot a povre gent.
612 Deu m'iert garant; bon confort ai.
Quanque faire me pues, ore me fai.'
Quant l'entent Decius Cesar,
Por poi ne muert d'ire et d'eschar.
616 Dunc le fait batre et tormenter
Et de grans fuz grans cous doner.
Saint Lorenz dit ens el torment:

'Jesus, Sire, graces t'en rent
620 De ceste joie que jeo ore ai
Et de cele que apruef arai!
Cruel tirant, or pues veer
Qu'en mon tresor ai bon espeir;
624 Sus tes tormenz ai ja vitoire,
La paine que jeo sent m'est gloire.
Quanque tu fais, si m'est delit!'
Decius dunc s'escrie et dit:
628 'Tu es tot plain d'enchantemenz;
Par ceo sormontes nos tormenz.
Un altre torment ore avras.'
Dunc fait aporter *laminas*:
632 Ceo est mult orible torment,
Si cumme dient romaine gent;
Ceo sunt platines de fer granz.
Dunc les fait metre li tiranz
636 Ardantes al costé del saint.
Tot art et brusle quanque ataint.
Art lui les costés et le dos,
La char lui brusle tresque as os.
640 Dunc dit: 'Jesus Deus, verai rei,
Aiez, Sire, merci de mei!
Quant por ton nun acusé fui
Ne te neai, ains te conui;
644 Quant demanderent, tei regehi
Esse Jesum Filium Dei.
Tu es Jesus Deus, verai Peres,
Et de tot le mund Salveres.'
648 Decius veit que ses tormenz
Ne valent rien; mult est dolenz.
Les plateines fait oster
Et lui de la terre lever,
652 Et dit au barun saint Lorenz:
'En tei vei art d'enchantemenz.
Se tu mes tormenz destruit as
Par art mei ne decevras pas.
656 Tos les deus jur que jeo aour
Que morir te ferai a dolor,

Se tu mun deu plus tost n'aoures,
De sacrefisse ne l'honores.'
660 Saint Lorenz dit: 'Torment ne dot,
Tei et ton deu guerpis del tot.
Quanque faire veus, tost le fai.
El nun Jesus le recevrai.'
664 Decius l'ot, mult est iriez.
Idunc l'unt tost despoillez,
De *plunbatis* l'unt debatu.
Dirai vos quel torment ceo fu:
668 Unes coroies qui sunt quarees,
A clous de plun soudé plummees.
D'icest le batent asprement,
N'a menbre qui ne soit tot samglent.
672 Par tot le cors lui funt granz plaies,
Parfundes, horibles et laies.
La ou il est si angoissous
Dunc dist: 'Damnedeu glorious,
676 Sire, receif mon esperit.'
Dunt oent une vois del ciel qui dit:
'Greignor estrif te sunt deu
Que tu n'en as encore eu.'
680 Et Decius la voiz entent;
Dunt dit: 'Ohi, romaine gent,
Oez cum la voiz del deable
Conforte ici cest mescreable.
684 Il ne dote ne deu ne mei,
Ne il ne crient prince ne rei;
Tant par est plain d'enchantemenz
Ne crient maus, ne tormenz.
688 Pernez le mei, sel me batez,
De toz tormenz le tormentez!'

(ii) Lawrence on the gridiron.

Sus le greil, la ou il gist
En rent merci a Jesu Crist.
A cest vers a bien entendu:
'Passames par eve et par fu,

872 En refrigerie nos menas,
    A tei en rendun *gratias*.'
    Valerien qui prevost fu
    Dit al saint: 'Ou sunt li fu
876 Que tu a nos deus prametoies
    Quant deis que tu les ardroies?'
    Et sain Lorenz dunc lui respunt
    Et dit as princes qui iloc sunt:
880 'Ohi, chetif maleuré
    De desverie forsené!
    Et n'avés vos dunc entendu
    Que nule ardor n'ai d'icest fu?
884 Ne jeo nel sent n'en char, n'en os,
    Ains m'est frigerie et repos.'
    Tuit icil qui iloc esteient,
    Hisdor et grant pité aveient
888 De la crualté Decii
    Qui vif le fait rostir issi.
    Dunc dist saint Lorenz en riant
    O simple vult, o bel semblant:
892 'Deu, tei en puisse jeo loer
    Qui ci me deignas conforter.'
    Ovre les oils et dunc si dit
    Decio que devant lui vit:
896 'Chaitif, l'altre part car tornez:
    Mangez deça, quit est assez!'
    Glorie et grace a Deu en rent
    Et dit: '*Pater* Omnipotent,
900 Jesu Crist, a tei graces rent,
    Qui m'as doné ceste memoire
    Que envers tei deservi ai,
    Si qu'a tes portes entrerai.'
904 Et li sains cum out ceo dit
    A Deu tramet son esperit.
    Dreit al ciel vait l'alme del saint.
    Le cors sus le greil remaint.

INDEXES OF PROPER NAMES

The references are to lines in the editions used in this volume.

The Life of St Catherine

Alexandria, 63, 133, 1865

Barking, Benedictine Abbey (Essex), home of Clemence of Barking, 2691

Catherine, St, 138, 376, 1335, 1827, etc.

Clemence, the Christian name of the author of the *Life of St Catherine*, 2690

Constantine, Constantine the Great (Roman emperor, AD 306–37), 57

Constantius, the father of the Emperor Constantine, 55

Cursates, Maxentius' provost, 2012

God, 28, 147, 158, 164, etc.

Helen, the mother of the Emperor Constantine (see n. 5), 56

Jesus (Christ), 239, 695, 697, 745, etc.

Jews, 748

Latin, 33

Mary, the Virgin, 1755

Maxentius, the rival of the Emperor Constantine (see n. 6), 61, 80, 644, 1494

Plato, 897

Porphiry, chief of military staff to the emperor, 1520, 1526, 1661, 1797, etc.

Rome, 53, 233

Sinai, Mount, 2628

Sybil, the, 903, 915 (see nn. 40, 42 and 43)

The Life of St Lawrence

Absalom, son of David, 42

Adam, 474

Agapitus, a deacon, 122, 235

Aristotle, 39

Artimius, a tribune, 248

Augustus, theatre of, (see n. 62) 764

Caesar [Augustus], Roman Emperor, 40

Capitoline Hill, the central hill of Rome's seven hills, 244

David, the Psalmist, 29, 155, 852

Decius (Caesar), Lawrence's persecutor (see n. 9), 95, 117, 130, 170, etc.

Ecclesiastes, a book of the Old Testament, 29

Eve, 474

Felicissimus, a deacon, 121, 235

God, 38, 62, 65, 83, etc.

Hippolytus, Valerian's lieutenant, 272, 319, 329, 354, etc.

Jesus (Christ), 111, 291, 298, 302, etc.

Jupiter, temple of, (see n. 60), 760

Justin, a priest, 752, 917, 921, 938

Lawrence, St, 62, 76, 125, 132, etc.

Lucillus, a convert to Christianity, 288, 293, 297

Mars, temple of, (see n. 21), 205, 209, 215

Olympias, wife of Philip II of Macedonia (see n. 61), 761

Olympias, baths of, Roman baths (see n. 61), 761.

Romans, 690

Romanus, a convert to Christianity, 707, 728

Rome, 86, 94, 108, 128, 762

Salaria, the gate where Romanus was beheaded, 743

Sallust, palace of (Sallust was a Roman Historian 86–34 BC; see n. 62), 765

Samson, the Biblical hero, 41

Sixtus, St (Sixtus II, Pope AD 257–8), 85, 93, 106, 125, etc.

Tiberius, (Roman Emperor, AD 14–37), 571, 910

Tiberius, palace of, 571, 910

Tiburtine Gate, (see n. 75), 924, 927

Valerian, the provost of Decius provost (see n. 28), 266, 271, 383, 386, etc.

Veranus, field of, the field located beside the Via Tiburtina (see n. 76), 928

MEDIEVAL LITERATURE
IN EVERYMAN

The Canterbury Tales
GEOFFREY CHAUCER
*The complete medieval text with
translations*
£4.99

The Vision of Piers Plowman
WILLIAM LANGLAND
edited by A. V. C. Schmidt
*The only complete edition of the
B-Text available*
£6.99

**Sir Gawain and the Green
Knight, Pearl, Cleanness,
Patience**
edited by J. J. Anderson
*Four major English medieval
poems in one volume*
£5.99

Arthurian Romances
CHRÉTIEN DE TROYES
translated by D. D. R. Owen
*Classic tales from the father of
Arthurian romance*
£5.99

**Everyman and Medieval
Miracle Plays**
edited by A. C. Cawley
*A fully representative selection
from the major play cycles*
£4.99

Anglo-Saxon Poetry
edited by S. A. J. Bradley
*An anthology of prose translations
covering most of the surviving
poetry of early medieval literature*
£6.99

Six Middle English Romances
edited by Maldwyn Mills
Tales of heroism and piety
£4.99

**Ywain and Gawain,
Sir Percyvell of Gales,
The Anturs of Arther**
edited by Maldwyn Mills
*Three Middle English romances
portraying the adventures of
Gawain*
£5.99

**The Birth of Romance:
An Anthology**
translated by Judith Weiss
*The first-ever English translation
of fascinating Anglo-Norman
romances*
£4.99

The Piers Plowman Tradition
edited by Helen Barr
*Four medieval poems of political
and religious dissent – available
together for the first time*
£5.99

All books are available from your local bookshop or direct from:
Littlehampton Book Services Cash Sales, 14 Eldon Way, Lineside Estate,
Littlehampton, West Sussex BN17 7HE (*prices are subject to change*)

To order any of the books, please enclose a cheque (in sterling) made payable to
Littlehampton Book Services, or phone your order through with credit card details (Access,
Visa or Mastercard) on 01903 721596 (24 hour answering service) stating card number
and expiry date. (*Please add £1.25 for package and postage to the total of your order.*)

In the USA, for further information and a complete catalogue call 1-800-526-2778

SAGAS AND OLD ENGLISH LITERATURE
IN EVERYMAN

Egils Saga
translated by Christine Fell
*A gripping story of Viking exploits
in Iceland, Norway and Britain*
£4.99

Edda
SNORRI STURLUSON
*The first complete English
translation of this important
Icelandic text*
£5.99

Anglo-Saxon Prose
edited by Michael Swanton
*Popular tales of Anglo-Saxon
England, written by kings, scribes
and saints*
£4.99

**The Fljotsdale Saga and
The Droplaugarsons**
translated by Eleanor Howarth
and Jean Young
*A brilliant portrayal of life and
times in medieval Iceland*
£3.99

Anglo-Saxon Poetry
translated by S. A. J. Bradley
*An anthology of prose translations
covering most of the surviving
poetry of early medieval literature*
£6.99

**Fergus of Galloway: Knight of
King Arthur**
GUILLAME LE CLERC
translated by D. D. R. Owen
*Essential reading for students
of Arthurian romance*
£3.99

**Three Arthurian Romances
from Medieval France**
translated and edited by
Ross G. Arthur
Caradoc, The Knight with the
Sword *and* The Perilous
Graveyard — *poems of the Middle
Ages for modern readers*
£5.99

All books are available from your local bookshop or direct from:
Littlehampton Book Services Cash Sales, 14 Eldon Way, Lineside Estate,
Littlehampton, West Sussex BN17 7HE (*prices are subject to change*)

To order any of the books, please enclose a cheque (in sterling) made payable to
Littlehampton Book Services, or phone your order through with credit card details (Access,
Visa or Mastercard) on 01903 721596 (24 hour answering service) stating card number
and expiry date. (*Please add £1.25 for package and postage to the total of your order.*)

In the USA, for further information and a complete catalogue call 1-800-526-2778

PHILOSOPHY AND RELIGIOUS WRITING
IN EVERYMAN

Modern Philosophy of Mind
edited by William Lyons
This unique anthology of classic readings in philosophy of mind over the last hundred years includes the writings of William James and Ludwig Wittgenstein
£6.99

Selected Writings
WILLIAM JAMES
Taking writings from James's most famous works, this edition is a comprehensive and unique selection
£6.99

The Prince and Other Political Writings
NICCOLÒ MACHIAVELLI
A clinical analysis of the dynamics of power, set in the context of Machiavelli's early political writings
£4.99

Ethics
SPINOZA
Spinoza's famous discourse on the power of understanding
£5.99

The World as Will and Idea
ARTHUR SCHOPENHAUER
New translation of abridged text, Schopenhauer's major work and key text of modern philosophy
£7.99

Utilitarianism, On Liberty, Considerations on Representative Government
J. S. MILL
Three radical works which transformed political science
£5.99

A Discourse on Method, Meditations, and Principles
RENÉ DESCARTES
Takes the theory of mind over matter into a new dimension
£5.99

An Essay Concerning Human Understanding
JOHN LOCKE
A central work in the development of modern philosophy
£5.99

Philosophical Writings
FRANCIS HUTCHESON
Comprehensive selection of Hutcheson's most influential writings
£6.99

Women Philosophers
edited by Mary Warnock
The great subjects of philosophy handled by women spanning four centuries, including Simone de Beauvoir and Iris Murdoch
£6.99

All books are available from your local bookshop or direct from:
Littlehampton Book Services Cash Sales, 14 Eldon Way, Lineside Estate,
Littlehampton, West Sussex BN17 7HE (*prices are subject to change*)

To order any of the books, please enclose a cheque (in sterling) made payable to *Littlehampton Book Services*, or phone your order through with credit card details (Access, Visa or Mastercard) on 01903 721596 (24 hour answering service) stating card number and expiry date. (*Please add £1.25 for package and postage to the total of your order.*)

In the USA, for further information and a complete catalogue call 1-800-526-2778

WOMEN'S WRITING
IN EVERYMAN

Poems and Prose
CHRISTINA ROSSETTI
A collection of her writings, poetry and prose, published to mark the centenary of her death
£5.99

Women Philosophers
edited by Mary Warnock
The great subjects of philosophy handled by women spanning four centuries, including Simone de Beauvoir and Iris Murdoch
£6.99

Glenarvon
LADY CAROLINE LAMB
A novel which throws light on the greatest scandal of the early nineteenth century – the infatuation of Caroline Lamb with Lord Byron
£6.99

Women Romantic Poets
1780 – 1830: **An Anthology**
edited by Jennifer Breen
Hidden talent from the Romantic era rediscovered
£5.99

Memoirs of the Life of Colonel Hutchinson
LUCY HUTCHINSON
One of the earliest pieces of women's biographical writing, of great historic and feminist interest
£6.99

The Secret Self 1: Short Stories by Women
edited by Hermione Lee
'A superb collection' The Guardian
£4.99

The Age of Innocence
EDITH WHARTON
A tale of the conflict between love and tradition by one of America's finest women novelists
£4.99

Frankenstein
MARY SHELLEY
A masterpiece of Gothic terror in its original 1818 version
£3.99

The Life of Charlotte Brontë
ELIZABETH GASKELL
A moving and perceptive tribute by one writer to another
£4.99

Victorian Women Poets
1830 – 1900
edited by Jennifer Breen
A superb anthology of the era's finest female poets
£5.99

Female Playwrights of the Restoration: Five Comedies
edited by Paddy Lyons
Rediscovered literary treasure in a unique selection
£5.99

All books are available from your local bookshop or direct from:
Littlehampton Book Services Cash Sales, 14 Eldon Way, Lineside Estate,
Littlehampton, West Sussex BN17 7HE *(prices are subject to change)*

To order any of the books, please enclose a cheque (in sterling) made payable to
Littlehampton Book Services, or phone your order through with credit card details (Access,
Visa or Mastercard) on 01903 721596 (24 hour answering service) stating card number
and expiry date. *(Please add £1.25 for package and postage to the total of your order.)*

In the USA, for further information and a complete catalogue call 1-800-526-2778

POETRY
IN EVERYMAN

Amorous Rites: Elizabethan Erotic Verse
edited by Sandra Clark
Erotic and often comic poems dealing with myths of transformation and erotic interaction between humans and gods
£4.99

Selected Poems
JOHN KEATS
An excellent selection of the poetry of one of the principal figures of the Romantic movement
£6.99

Poems and Prose
CHRISTINA ROSSETTI
A new collection of her writings, poetry and prose, marking the centenary of her death
£5.99

Poems and Prose
P. B. SHELLEY
The essential Shelley in one volume
£5.99

Silver Poets of the Sixteenth Century
edited by Douglas Brooks-Davies
An exciting and comprehensive collection
£6.99

Complete English Poems
JOHN DONNE
The father of metaphysical verse in this highly-acclaimed collection
£6.99

Complete English Poems, Of Education, Areopagitica
JOHN MILTON
An excellent introduction to Milton's poetry and prose
£6.99

Women Romantic Poets 1780–1830: An Anthology
edited by Jennifer Breen
Hidden talent from the Romantic era rediscovered
£5.99

Selected Poems
D. H. LAWRENCE
An authoritative selection spanning the whole of Lawrence's literary career
£4.99

The Poems
W. B. YEATS
Ireland's greatest lyric poet surveyed in this ground-breaking edition
£7.99

All books are available from your local bookshop or direct from:
Littlehampton Book Services Cash Sales, 14 Eldon Way, Lineside Estate,
Littlehampton, West Sussex BN17 7HE (*prices are subject to change*)

To order any of the books, please enclose a cheque (in sterling) made payable to
Littlehampton Book Services, or phone your order through with credit card details (Access,
Visa or Mastercard) on 01903 721596 (24 hour answering service) stating card number
and expiry date. (*Please add £1.25 for package and postage to the total of your order.*)

In the USA, for further information and a complete catalogue call 1-800-526-2778